HOW TO TALK JEWISH

HOW TO TALK JEWISH

JACKIE MASON

WITH IRA BERKOW

St. Martin's Press   New York

ISBN 0-312-05445-9

10 9 8 7 6 5 4 3 2

HOW TO TALK JEWISH

INTRODUCTION

↕ I ↕

My family always spoke Yiddish. It was the first language I ever heard and it was the first language I spoke. In my neighborhood, everybody spoke Yiddish. I didn't know that anybody spoke English in this country until I was old enough to go to the movies. When I went to the movies, I heard people talk in English, and I thought they were in the wrong country. "Who are these people?" I wondered.

Everybody in the neighborhood spoke Jewish—that's what Jews commonly call Yiddish. I thought Jewish was English at the time. I didn't know there was an English language. Nobody ever heard it. If somebody talked English it looked like he had come from a foreign country. He had to be a spy trying to infiltrate our neighborhood. Otherwise why would he be talking a foreign language?

I was born in Sheboygan, Wisconsin, in 1934, and by the time I was five years old my family had moved to New York City. My father, who was a rabbi, wanted the whole family to be able to go to *yeshivas*—Jewish schools—and there were no advanced *yeshivas* in a small town like Sheboygan. He wanted to make sure that my three brothers and my two sisters all had a religious education. He wanted all of his sons to be educated in the orthodoxy that it takes to become a rabbi. It was my father's blind ambition that each of his sons would become a rabbi.

Nobody asked my opinion. I couldn't say I disagreed because if a fight broke out with him I didn't stand a chance. And I couldn't leave the house because nobody was renting apartments to five-year-old children. And there was no place for me to make enough money to pay the rent. So I had to go along with what I was told. And we moved to the Lower East Side of New York and lived on Henry Street and Rutgers Street and Norfolk Street and all those streets around there.

My parents still spoke Yiddish even when they learned a little English. They were both born in Minsk, Russia, and in the 1920s they emigrated to New York. But there were so many rabbis on the Lower East Side that it was impossible for my father to make a living. A Jewish refugee organization that arranged for Jews to move to towns and cities in America helped my father find an opening in a town in which a Jewish community needed a rabbi.

My family moved to Sheboygan—and that's where I became the first boy in my family ever born in America. Then, my family moved back to New York. All of my parents' friends in New York spoke Yiddish, and there was such an enclave of ghetto-ized Jewish atmosphere and religious atmosphere that they dealt only with each other. So there was little effort to attempt to speak English. There was no purpose in it. After all, the whole neighborhood was populated by refugees. The grocer didn't talk English, the shoemaker didn't talk English, the butcher didn't talk English. So why learn it?

The only reason that older Jews began talking English was that eventually their children went to public schools and then to college, and when they came home they would speak English. That was the way the parents picked up the language.

This has been going on in America now for several generations. This is probably the third generation that is practically no longer dealing in Yiddish. So Yiddish is definitely a dying language. The next generation will be speaking it even less. Most areas in which Yiddish was commonly spoken in America have been virtually wiped out, though it's estimated that four million people around the world still speak it. (It was the first language of some 11 million before the Holocaust.) But in America there is almost nothing left of the Yiddish press or the Yiddish theater.

Yiddish began in central Europe, primarily in Germany, around the twelfth century. You can still hear the influence of German in Yiddish, and the similarity between the two languages. But Yiddish is a blend of numerous languages, and wherever Jews were living, they tacked on words from the different countries and languages. So you have derivative words from such languages as Russian and Polish, and even English. Jews clung to the language because it helped them identify with each other more closely. Their language was the thing that made them feel close; it was something they shared. It formed a bond between them. As Jews assimilated they needed Yiddish less, and began concentrating on the language of their country.

Today Jews and others interested in language are trying to salvage Yiddish by studying it in colleges, but everybody knows that when you study something in a college you don't use it again after college. You might as well never have learned it because it serves no purpose. Like Latin or Sanskrit. There will be three intellectuals doing research in some ivory tower university three hundred years from now, telling you what a great language Yiddish once was.

If Yiddish dies out, it will be a great loss. It's a colorful language and a very dynamic form of expression. And that's why to this day I use it. It is pictorially more interesting, I think, than English. It tells you a whole story and it has a comedic sound. It has ramifications and intonations that you don't get in English.

Yiddish is one of the most expressive languages in the world. It has sounds that match the meaning of the words—for example the word *geshmak*, which means *tasty*. It's said with virtually a smacking of the lips, as though you've just taken a bite of a delicious corned beef sandwich. Or how about the word *burtchen*, which means someone doesn't stop complaining, griping, or bothering you. When you say *"Burtchen, burtchen, burtchen,"* it *sounds* like someone's bothering you. It sounds like stupid sounds are coming from the other person.

Yiddish sayings or proverbs often have picturesque images as well, like *"Ahfen ganef brent dos hittel,"* which is translated literally: "On the head of a thief burns his hat." It means a person has a guilty conscience and that a guilty person is always sensitive. His head is always hot with anxiety.

⇓ **II** ⇓

There's an amazing connection in Yiddish with the words and the emotions they describe. If you say *"Chossen"*—with the hard "kh" for "ch"—and *"kalleh,"* with the softer "k," you could guess which is the man and which is the woman by the sounds of the words. *Chossen* is the groom and *kalleh* is the bride. *Kalleh* somehow has a feminine sound, a gentler, more delicate sound. *Chossen* has a harder sound.

Yiddish has vivid words for beauty and ugliness, for love and hate, for kindness and harassment. It has lovely words for sweetness, for happiness, for joy. And it has great deceptive words for derision, for abuse, for cursing, etc. . . . There's a saying, *"Zol dir vaksen tzibbeles fun pupik,"* meaning, "Onions should grow from your navel." The analogy to an onion in your stomach is laughable in itself, and it draws a picture. An onion is a ridiculous vegetable. How many vegetables can make you cry and burn in your stomach? You're talking to a person who is eating a sandwich with an onion in it and he's crying. You have to laugh because he's not crying from something tragic. It's a tear jerker without a harmful effect. So you're not wishing a person that much harm when you're talking about a ludicrous object that makes you cry. But you're not wishing him happiness, either.

Yiddish is so rich that it has been picked up and adopted in other languages. There are some five hundred Yiddish and Hebrew words in the English dictionary. There's everything from *meshuggener* (crazy person) and *tochkes* (someone's rear end) to *schatchen* (matchmaker) and *mazel tov* (good luck). The words have so much taste and sound and smell and feel, they are so full of images, that Americans began to adopt them.

In Yiddish a question even sounds more like a question because of the more intense rhythms. *"Vu gayst du?"* which means "Where are you going?" It's something like the rhythms Italians have in their language. American speech, for the most part, is flat. There aren't a lot of intonations. It is not emotionally expressive.

Blacks, though, speak English the way Jews use Yiddish. When blacks talk there's a lot of rhythm in their speech, a lot of emotion in the highs and lows of their voices. "What's happenin'?" is as packed with speech intonations as "Vu gayst du?" It's almost musical when you hear a Jew or a black person or an Italian speak. I think those cultures are given much more to expressing themselves emotionally than are Americans or the English. When you get emotional you're more likely to find it as much in the sound of the language as in the use of the word itself. All of a sudden the sounds go up and down in so many different directions that you can *feel* the words as much as hear them.

It seems in English that you have to prove that you're not emotional in order to have class. Intensity and expressiveness are considered crude in English. The more class a person has, the more money he makes, the higher the level of his society, the cooler he is and the flatter his speech becomes.

By the time he's reached the height of elitism, his speech is so monotonous and low key that you can't understand a word he's saying. Emotion is somehow the opposite of culture and class to an American. To him an emotional expression proves somehow that he can't control himself, that he's lost his ability to restrain himself. He is somehow never schooled enough or trained enough to learn how to act like a gentleman, so he has to learn to mumble in a monotone. Then he's considered the most cultured person in the neighborhood.

In the lower classes of society, where a lot of people are untutored and uncultured and even illiterate, you hear people talking with a lot of emotion. Their speech is dynamic. I think that that's why on television now we see so many ethnic or low-income situation comedies. I think that that's why Jackie Gleason and *The Honeymooners*, for example, have been so enduring and are so loved. People enjoy seeing people who are different, who are honest and able to be in touch with their emotions and express more of their emotions. But before you know it, it's embarrassing to scream, it's not nice to cry, it's terrible to yell, it's horrible to talk, it's tasteless to move. But if you hear an ethnic family from Brooklyn, you hear and feel fireworks. It's no accident that the Honeymooners lived in Brooklyn.

Jews have always been very free in terms of expressiveness. That's why Jews were always among the best comedians, and still are. Jews always felt alienated from the rest of the world and they had no other way of fighting back against that feeling of alienation except through their humor. They were always a defenseless, helpless minority and they had to hide their true feelings in society at large because they were so suppressed. Their only outlet was to express themselves in the privacy of their homes or in their relationships. So to relieve their frustrations, to find ventilation for their emotions, they argued among themselves and fought among themselves and screamed and laughed among themselves.

Humor has been one avenue of escape for Jews throughout history. They managed to find humor in the most tragic circumstances. That's why Jews, until Israel came about, were never known as fighters. Jews knew that things were so stacked against them by the countries in which they were living that the only sure way they could never win a fight was by fighting. So they had to find ways of winning the fight by avoiding it, outsmarting their opponent, outmaneuvering him, coddling him, lying to him, hiding from him. Anything except fighting, because he was so out-numbered, so outmanned, so outarmed. The whole thing became a battle of wits and a battle of tricks and games.

If a cop catches you speeding for example you're not going to fight with the cop. You try to see how you can outsmart the cop, outmaneuver him, talk him out of the ticket, try to find his weakness. That's what Jews did. All the others were the policemen, and the Jew was always trying to avoid them. The whole world was the enemy to the Jew. A Jew was always the guy who just got caught by a cop for speeding.

If a Jew was ever attacked, he couldn't call a cop because the cop was always on the other side. The Jew was always the victim, from both sides. In such circumstances, humor always helped give the Jew perspective and a sense of balance. Humor is a way to maintain your equilibrium in the face of misery. It's the saving grace for a person who feels so overwhelmed that he has to find a way to survive by laughing at misery. It's basically the avoidance of reality. It's a way of creating a different world for yourself, as drinking does for some gentiles. It's another way to change the subject.

A Jew doesn't drink much because then he'd really be at a disadvantage against his enemies. He has to stay sober to keep his head, to outwit the cossacks, the gestapo, the secret police—even his own neighbors who might try to do him in.

That's why a lot of Jews became great fiction writers and great musicians and composers. That's why they wrote such stories and fables and poems and humor. And that's why they composed great songs and were some of the best pianists and violinists in the world. Jews were always having to create a world to live in to replace the real world that they had to deal with. Yiddish helped them build their world. And good health to it!

A Broch:
pronounced, ah-BROOKH

This is a curse, a plague. Like "Damn it!" but more so. A *broch* is a way of expressing disgust, misery, disaster. If a guy wants to tell you he's miserable, he's nauseated, he's overwhelmed, he's disgusted, he's at his wit's end, he's heard the end of it, he wants to give up, he wants to run away, he wants to get out of town, he wants to destroy himself, it's all over, there's no end in sight, there's no way to get out of it, all of this can be said in one phrase, "*Oy, a broch.*"

A gentile would have to find five thousand ways of letting you know how he's feeling. A Jew just says, "*Oy, a broch,*" and you know that this guy can't take anymore and you'd better get out of his way. Because the next thing is murder.

And *a broch* can range from the tailor fixing your pants too short to the death of a relative. It's an all-purpose word.

A Gezunt Dir in Pupik:
pronounced, ah Geh-SOONT dear en POOHP-ik

This is a blessing, and means good health to your belly button, but the general meaning is that your whole system should stay healthy and be in good shape. It's a colorful, preposterous way of making a profound point: Because your life started with your belly button, it's the center of your entire being.

To wish health to your belly button has a lot of meaning because Jews are always concerned about good health. When a Jew says "goodbye," he never just says "goodbye," but also wishes *gezunt*, which is health, and that you should be strong and able to plant trees, to put up buildings, to cross streets faster than anybody, to sit longer, to climb higher, and to dance better.

You can't walk away from a Jew you've met on the street without listening to blessings upon blessings. Even if you've visited someone in his home for ten seconds, the blessings take an hour and a half. My mother used to follow you out the door and keep blessing you: "And God should give you more pillows, more quilts, more salt shakers, more sodium, more carbohydrates. God should give you more chairs, more tables, you should have more furniture to sit on, more food to eat, more forks to eat with, more feet to walk on, more places to go, more people to see . . ."

Jew have to protect each other from common problems as well as things nobody ever even heard of: "You shouldn't know from unhappiness, you shouldn't know from sadness. And even if you're hurt you shouldn't feel pain. And if you have the pain it should go away in a second. If somebody calls you names, you shouldn't hear. You shouldn't know from strong winds, from loud voices, from noisy rooms, from hysterical wives, from fat cockroaches, from slow trains, from jumpy elevators. You shouldn't know from anybody grabbing you, from anybody robbing you, from anybody chasing you, from anybody cursing you, from people screaming at you, from people looking at you.

"You should never know from a bad toenail, from a bad

tooth, from an earache, from a dirty finger, from a transplanted kidney, from tight shoes.

"You should only know from the best butcher, the best plumber, the best dentist, the best foot doctor. In case you walk to the store you should never know from swollen feet. In case you have to buy something you should never have trouble with your credit card. You should never know from a bad heart, and only your enemies should suffer from heartburn. You should never know from congestion. You should never suffer from irritation or constipation. You should never leave the house without Maalox.

"You should always have love in your heart, goodness in your soul, and you should only know from kindness, from love, from sex appeal.

"You should always have the best pound cake, you should never have static on your television set. The goodness of life should always be in your house. Your rich relatives should always know who you are, and your poor relatives should never be able to find you."

All of this comes when your belly button is healthy. When an Italian says goodbye, he wishes you only one thing— a long life. It's not like a Jew who is worried about your total well-being. An Italian is concerned that you're going to die not from bad health but from somebody killing you. That's why he always asks, "Is anybody bothering you?" He's going to protect you. You're not in jeopardy of just losing your health, you might also lose your life, or at least get your legs broken. So the Italian is always offering protection, and the protection is usually from himself because he hates it if somebody else would break your legs.

Jews don't offer you protection from people, they offer you protection from God. Jews deal only with God; that's how

Jews are different from other people. Jews convince themselves that if you can get God on your side, then you have nothing to worry about. They say, "God should protect you. God should give you health and happiness. May God be with you." They always start with God. "May God watch over you. May God help you climb the stairs. May God let you get proper rest." They're always trying to protect you from the wrath of God, not protecting you from the wrath of another human being.

Jews are always telling you in their blessings how long to live. Every Jew tells you you should live to be 120. But there's always a Jew who says you can live to 150. Some other Jew tops that. He says, "You should live forever. You should never die. Everybody should drop dead except you." It's always $3,000 worth of blessings for every two-cents' worth of conversation.

It's impossible to get away when a Jew is going on and on about blessings. And the older the Jew the more the blessings.

I never saw a gentile wish you good health and strength and happiness for three hours. Gentiles say, "I'll see you." Or, "So long." Or, "Best of luck to you." "Same to you." The best of luck is the most a gentile ever offers you. As for children and grandchildren, gentiles just wish each other luck. When a gentile says "Good luck," he thinks he includes everything and the case is closed. But a Jew is always wishing luck on the children and grandchildren and the great-grandchildren. They don't care if you have these children or not. They're wishing you luck just in case you have them, in case you know anybody else who has them.

When I see an old Jew, I don't even say hello. I take out a piece of paper and I read blessings: "Your aunt Harriet should be fine, your brother-in-law Max should be perfect . . ." Every time I see Jews, you can bet they ask each other how they are

12

for a second-and-a-half, then they go through the family.
"How are the children?"

"Good."

"Oh, fantastic!"

"I'm so happy to hear that."

"And how are the grandchildren?"

"Oh, fantastic!"

"How is the uncle?"

"Unbelievable!"

"And the nephew?"

"Oy, my God!"

They go through the list for an hour-and-a-half. Then they forget why they met in the first place, and turn around and go home.

A Gezunta Moid:
pronounced, ah Geh-SOON-teh moyd

It literally means "a healthy girl," but there is a connotation beyond that. It's a girl who looks so healthy she is capable of unbelievable things. It's said when you don't want to talk too dirty but you're still thinking about sex. A *gezunta moid* means, What she could do to you requires a lot of health to do.

It can also mean you'll lose your health if you get involved with her. She could kill twelve Jews like you in a second. Well-stacked is what you really mean when you say A *gezunta moid*. You're not admiring her health like a doctor. It's not because she was once sick and now she turned healthy. And

13

it's not that you saw, God forbid, that she was passing away from a disease. You're just thinking, Oh, boy, what all that health could do for me!

A Klug:
||||||||||||||||||||||||||
pronounced, ah-KLOHG

This is a curse, like *a broch*, but not as severe. You run for a full block and just miss a bus, and you slap your head. *Oy, a klug. Klug* means "woe." It's an exaggerated way of saying that you're overwhelmed by the problem. So it always has a humorous side to it because a Jew always knows that no matter how bad things get, he's going to come back and he's going to fight it his way. There's going to be another bus coming along, or he'll go to another street.

Even if your umbrella doesn't open in the rain, you know it's not the most serious thing in the world, but you have to get something off your chest, and so you say *Oy, a klug!* That takes in the weather, the umbrella, the guy who made the umbrella and your mother-in-law who bought you the umbrella for a Hanukkah present.

Another example is a guy tries to attack you on a dark street, and you hit him over the head with a pipe. He stays the same, but the pipe breaks. That's when you say, *Oy, a klug.*

14

A Makeh Unter Yenems Orem Iz Nit Shver Tsu Trogen:

pronounced, ah-MAKEH UN-ter YENEMS iz nit shver tsu TRO-gen

It literally means that another person's problems are not difficult for *you* to endure. Every other time someone says that he has a vicious toothache, the other person always says, "Don't worry, it'll go away." It's amazing how rational the other person is about your misery. A man says to someone, "I can't walk."

His friend always says, "What's the matter?"

"My foot hurts."

"So you'll walk a little less, it's not so terrible. Sitting is good for you."

If someone says his car isn't working, the response is, "Who says you have to ride in a car? Take a walk. What's wrong, you don't like the weather?"

A man says that he's passing away tomorrow. His friend tells him, "So what? In today's world, is life such a bargain? I'm still living and I've got nothing but misery. You're dying, but look how many problems you're saving. At least with what's going on in the world today, you should thank God that you're going. You don't have to hear about it."

Every time you're miserable, the other guy becomes a great philosopher. All of a sudden, the most brilliant philosophical statement in the world is expressed. It comes from a combination of happiness that it didn't happen to him and the fact that he really can't feel your pain. And so the great mind convinces himself that it's really not that big a problem.

15

A Shtuken Nisht in Harts:
pronounced, ah SHTU-ken nisht in HEARTS

It means "a stab in the heart" and it hurts like hell. It is anything that is a painful experience, a shocking, miserable memory. It happens every time a Jew passes a building that he could have bought twelve years ago for $1 million and learns that it's now worth $60 million. He just took a $59 million loss. That's *a shtuken nisht in harts.*

Other Examples:

A guy just got a divorce, and goes to the bank to take out some money and finds his wife has been there first.

You took a girl to Atlantic City and when you open the door of your hotel room you find somebody else in bed with her.

You send your son to college to become a doctor and he comes home and tells you he wants to be a hairdresser.

You fight tooth and nail to get your fiancée to sign a prenuptial agreement, and then you find out that you're the one with the money. That's when you slump in your chair and say "A *shtuken nisht in harts.*"

A Vue Shtet Geschreiber:
pronounced, ah voo shtet geh-SHRIBE-er

It means, "Where is it written? Who says it's so?" Any time someone makes a statement, and if you want to call him a liar without calling him a liar, you say, "Where does it say that? Where's the evidence for this story? Who says it has to be this way—why can't it be the other way?"

Most people can never admit that they're not sure. They give you a statement as something definite, as though it were carved in the Ten Commandments.

A father is supporting his children. The son is thirty-eight years old and he's asking the father for a weekly allowance. The father says, "Where is it written that I have to support you until you're thirty-eight years old? I could see it when you were nine, but thirty-eight?"

And where is it written that when you come home after 11:30 you have to account to your wife for every minute you've been out?

Where is it written that it can't take more than ten minutes to buy the newspaper and walk back home?

Where is it written that I have to take the dog for a walk?

Where is it written that just because everybody else uses deodorant, I'm not allowed to stink a little bit?

Where is it written that just because on a honeymoon everybody else makes love, I can't sit down and have lunch?

Where is it written that socks have to match?

Where is it written that you have to take your clothes off to have sex?

17

Who says you have to wear a shirt before you put on a tie?

People who question society, who question whatever is traditional, always ask the question, Where is it written? The most brilliant people in the world are always the ones who ask that question. They are the real doubters of tradition, who evaluate society on the most basic terms. They create new directions and new paths for society to go in. They think of ways to exist that no one ever thought of before. Think about the great inventors:

Just because everybody uses smoke signals, I can't use a telephone?

Just because everybody rides a horse, I can't invent a car?

Just because a bird flies, it means I can't? Where is it written?

Ahf Mir Gezogt:
pronounced, ahf Meer geh-ZOKHT

It translates roughly as "I wish I had that" or "It should only happen to me." If another man has a young, gorgeous girl, it's *"Ahf mir gezogt."* Or if someone else is making a better living than you or just bought a bigger car. It's a little less than total envy, total resentment, total hatred and jealousy. It's a little less than saying a person is *ongeshtupt*, or swollen with riches.

Ahf mir gezogt usually goes with a deep breath of exasperation and misery because it's not yours. "So how come I never got it? What did I do that I shouldn't deserve it?" It's

18

as if to say, "What a perverted sense of justice. No wonder Jews are suffering. No wonder a Jew can't get a decent break in this world. The world is upside down."

It can also apply to someone in a cash business. Like a restaurant owner or a waiter or someone who has a candy store. It's anybody who is making money and doesn't have to report it to the IRS, even if it's only a profit of thirty cents. Even a guy shining shoes. A man says to his friend, "You know something? It's a pathetic thing what a guy has to do to make a living." And the friend says, "But it's a cash business." And the first man shrugs his shoulders and says, "*Ahf mir gezogt.*"

When you don't want to get involved in guessing just how rich the other person is, it's because it hurts too much to guess, it's easier just to say, *Ahf mir gezogt.*

Ahfen Ganef Brent Dos Hittel:
pronounced, off-en gon-iff brehnt dohs HIT-tel

The literal translation is, "On the head of a thief burns his hat." It means that the person always feels guilty for something that he did or was thinking about doing. It's another way of saying that his head is aching from guilt, burning from sin, that his conscience is troubled.

He's a thief or a louse, and he knows he's been caught or might soon be caught or should be caught.

Like the guy who is hiding from the cops. No matter

where he sits, he thinks the guy next to him is about to arrest him. When the waiter comes over to give him a cup of coffee, he thinks it's really an FBI man in disguise. He's never comfortable no matter where he goes.

Sometimes his worry is justified, sometimes it's just paranoia.

He's driving a car and imagines that everyone thinks he stole it.

Whenever a husband comes home after 11:00, he starts to apologize to his wife. He says, "I did not." She says, "I didn't ask you."

Ahf Tsu Loches:
pronounced, ahf-tsoo-LOKH-ess

It literally means, "As fate would have it." It's as if by some grand design, something is beyond your control. Just my luck. I loan him all my money and, *ahf tsu loches*, he opens a store across the street. He wipes me out with my own money.

A guy says he wants to fix his nose. I recommend the surgeon and then, *ahf tsu loches*, the guy runs off with my wife.

As soon as I start out on a trip, I run out of gas. I park the car and, *ahf tsu loches*, three guys steal the motor, they steal the radio, and they take the front seat, too.

I finally get a pretty girl in a dark movie theater and, *ahf tsu loches*, her mother sits down next to us. I finally get the girl in bed and—what happens?—the bed collapses. We fix the bed and, *ahf tsu loches*, a flood comes in.

Alter Kocker:
pronounced, OLL-ter KOCK-er

An *alter kocker* is a man who can no longer do something that he once could. He's an old guy, over the hill, past his prime.

In literal terms, an *alter kocker* is from German and means "old defecator." It doesn't sound very nice in translation, but it's a common expression, and sounds gentler and more humorous in Yiddish conversation. Its sense is usually of someone who is inept at whatever he's trying to do. It often has to do with forgetfulness. As soon as somebody says hello to a man but can't remember his name, the other guy says, "You *alter kocker*." The other guy can't admit to himself that he's not too well liked, or not worth remembering. So he blames you.

Another thing an *alter kocker* is famous for is playing golf. There are certain activities that are recognizable for old people that only an *alter kocker* gets involved in and golf is one. A man wants to go for a walk, but he doesn't want to feel like he's just going for a plain walk, so he takes a stick with him. He doesn't have to do anything, but now he convinces himself that he's an athlete. He can feel young. If he takes a walk, he holds a stick and he swings it. He doesn't remember if there was a ball there or not. It's not that important. He misses the ball by three feet but he's still happy.

An *alter kocker* is also someone who had sex a month ago and his wife says, "Don't you think it's about time we got into bed together?" An *alter kocker* is someone who could have sex, but not more than once a month, and even then he can't do it if there's a girl there. A girl just keeps getting in his way.

21

Balagoleh:

pronounced, bah-la-GOH-leh

Originally, this was someone who drove a wagon. Now he's a truck driver or a cab driver. It was always a derisive term and it applied to a guy who was considered to have gotten nowhere in life. Unfortunately, a truck driver was often one who was thought to be crude, who had no class, had no manners, was not gracious, not delicate, not sophisticated, was vulgar. But it's a bad rap on truck drivers, and I think it's bad taste to give him this connotation.

If you call a guy a *balagoleh*, you're really saying he's the equivalent of a person at the lowest economic level. But a truck driver today is not at the lowest economic level anymore. He's a respectable citizen with a relatively good union job who makes as much money today as most of the people in professional jobs. But there is still the stigma of being a truck driver and a cab driver.

If you're in the Catskills and meet the average New York cab driver who is there on vacation and ask him what he does for a living, he'll never admit he's a cab driver. He'll tell you, "I'm in the transportation business" or "I'm in communications." He'll find some kind of profession that sounds high-class without being a total liar. It's a little too self-conscious to say, "I'm a bank president." That has nothing to do with his real job. But if he says he's in the transportation business, or even communications, he's verging on the truth to a degree.

Taxi drivers now make a comfortable living, but the guy driving the taxi is still embarrassed by his job. That's why, whenever you get into a cab, the driver always has an apologetic speech to make. But while others might be comfortable driving a taxi cab nowadays a Jew still isn't.

You'll notice that a gentile who drives a cab is a cab driver, but not a Jew. The first thing every Jewish cab driver says is, "You think I need this?" I hear this from every taxi driver. "This is not my regular business. I just sold a luncheonette and moved from Philadelphia. I just gave up a business in Pittsburgh. I could open four more businesses tomorrow. You think I want to bother with this? I only do this to help out my brother-in-law."

Jewish cab drivers are always helping out somebody. If you ask, "Who are you helping out?" they'll say, "I don't remember who the guy was who owned the taxi. I wasn't busy that day so I just started driving. You think I know why? I don't need this. I piss away money like this in ten minutes; it means nothing to me. You think I want a tip? You think I care about it? Who wants it? A lousy dollar to a guy like me? A man in my position, do you think I need a dollar? All right, I'll take it. Do you think after all, I want to hurt your feelings?"

Bashert:
pronounced, bah-SHAIRT

t means "fate," and a very typical word for Jewish people because they like to think that things are all *bashert*, or a product solely of fate. When people don't have an answer to why something happened, they say it's *bashert*. They romanticize, for example, the whole idea of a guy and a girl meeting. It was fate that put them together. Gentiles

23

also like to think that relationships come from fate, but they don't put quite as much stock in it as Jews do. To find the right mate, gentiles think you have to travel around a lot, meet people, join three hundred singles groups, vacation with Club Med, attend a matching session, go to another group, then to a singles bar. Finally, you meet someone. And that is fate.

Gentiles don't talk so much about fate because they work too hard to find the right person. They want to attribute it to their intelligence. They know so much about psychology that they understand how to evaluate a person.

In the old days in Europe, Jews didn't go anyplace. You met a person because there wasn't anyone else to meet. Jews lived in a very small town, called a *shtetl*. Someone put you together with someone and it was all artificially arranged. The person who did this was called a *schatchen*, or matchmaker. And the families had to convince themselves that these two people really belonged together.

There was no reason for this couple to be together. They didn't pick each other out. There was no other way to justify the stupidity of these two people having nothing in common having to live the rest of their lives together, so people told themselves that it was God's way. "It's *bashert*." When there's no freedom of choice, you have to blame it on God.

Nowadays, if your daughter marries a guy you can't stand, in order to make yourself comfortable with it you say it's *bashert*. They have to bring God into it to find an excuse for accepting it. You don't want to say she's an idiot, or the marriage stinks or the thing won't last or it's the dumbest thing you ever saw. You try to prevent it until the wedding day, and every inch of the way you're complaining and fighting and screaming and threatening to kill, plunder, and murder. But she marries him anyway, and you say, it's *bashert*, it was the will of God. The will of God means you fought like hell and you lost.

It's also *bashert* that I can never get a decent sandwich in this restaurant. Or that there's a piece of meat stuck in my tooth and I can't find a toothpick.

It's *bashert* when a guy crosses the street without looking both ways and gets hit by a truck. He can't admit it's his fault when he has an accident. So he always says "It was from heaven." It was always God who did it to him. God had nothing to do with it because if you were looking, this accident never would have happened. But he says, God wants it and you can't fight God. God is supposed to watch the traffic for you. But what right did you have to give God the assignment of watching out for the next car? So it's *bashert* because it was God's business but he wasn't paying attention.

Billik:
pronounced, BILL-ick

It means "cheap" or "inexpensive." It's usually regarding something that you got a good price on. It's used in the saying, *Billik vi borsht!*, which means "cheap as beet soup." The greatest fear a Jew has is that he should pay a regular price for anything. He doesn't know what he paid for it, but it has to be a bargain. And if it's a bargain, he got it *billik*.

A Jew says, "I paid $300 for a dress." His friend says, "$300 for a dress? You spent a fortune!" The first Jew says, "But it sold for $500." The friend says, "Oh, what a deal!"

25

Now he's thrilled. Fabulous. You saved $200. Thank God. *Billik vi borsht.* They don't care how much you spend, it's how much you saved.

Jewish wives are always saving their husbands millions of dollars this way. The wives tell their husbands that they're making them rich with all the money they're saving them on bargains. Meanwhile the husband is becoming so rich from her that he's walking around the neighborhood with holes in his shoes.

Bobbeh Meisseh:
pronounced, BOH-beh MY-seh

It literally means "grandmother's tale," but can also be translated as "old wives' tale." Jews use it to express to someone that they're full of baloney. It's the bluntest way a Jew has of calling a man a liar, a phoney, a contemptuous lout.

A guy says, "I just won the lottery." Of course he didn't win the lottery. So it's a *bobbeh meisseh.*

Or when your brother-in-law sitting next to you in a restaurant claims he's still living. That's another *bobbeh meisseh*, because when the check came, he stopped moving and breathing.

A politician is behind in the polls and says, "Polls don't count." His opponent says, "It's a *bobbeh meisseh.*" But when he's ahead, the same politician says, "Can't you see the polls? They're totally accurate." Then the other guy comes out with, "Ha! Another *bobbeh meisseh.*"

Every time a wife finds lipstick on her husband's collar, he always has a story. That's a sure way to find out what a *bobbeh meisseh* means. Or a wife confronts her husband with why he has a girl's telephone number in his book. He says, "She's my assistant's partner." Or "My father-in-law's mother." Or "His uncle's aunt." The man is stuck and he doesn't care what he says to try to get out of it. He says it as fast as possible and with as many explanations as possible. But it is so obvious that it immediately becomes a *bobbeh meisseh*.

Whenever a husband is caught by his wife looking at another woman, he comes up with a fast string of *bobbeh meissehs*. She says, "Why are you staring at her so hard?" He says, "I'm not staring. Who's staring? I'm looking at her dress. I'm amazed." She says, "Amazed at what?" He says, "That short skirts are coming back again. I didn't know that. I wasn't looking at her. I was looking at that skirt." She says, "How come you were trying to look all the way up her legs?" He says, "Legs? What looking at her legs? This girl's got legs? She's got a skirt. I was just noticing the skirt." The wife says, "No, you weren't." The husband says, "I was just looking at how fat she is in that skirt. I was shocked at how much weight she's gained." The wife says, "But you never saw her before." He says, "That shocks me even more, that I should notice it!"

Another *bobbeh meisseh* is that you live twenty minutes from the city. Every Jew in the world lives twenty minutes from the city. Every time they want to take you to their house, every time somebody invites you out, and you say, "I'm sorry, I'm busy, it's too far for me to travel." That's when you find out that they live "just twenty minutes from the city." Even a helicopter can't get there in twenty minutes. You can't make a phone call there in twenty minutes, but somehow your car will get there in twenty minutes. And every time you get

27

there, it takes an hour and a half. And they always say the same thing: "You must have hit a lot of traffic. How much traffic was there?" You say, "There was no traffic." They say, "That's it! You must have been surprised that there was no traffic so you were driving very slow."

You hear a *bobbeh meisseh* every time a cop stops a Jew driving a car. Now all of a sudden your mother's life isn't worth a nickel. "I'm going to my mother's funeral." Or a man will moan that his wife just had a heart attack or that one of his children just got hit by a tree that fell from lightning. If they'd tell such a story in any other circumstance, they'd be called the lowest bastard on the face of the earth. But in this situation, when a cop is about to write you out a ticket, every *bobbeh meisseh* you can think of is legitimate. "It's not that I don't want this ticket, I'd love to have this ticket, but I just got a paralytic stroke, my body is not really moving, my tongue is now caught in my esophagus, I just came back from a sex change operation, and I have to get home to rest."

But if you said these things any other time, you'd be considered a rotten person because Jews are very superstitious. They would knock on wood, because they'd be worried that it's an omen, it's terrible, and if God is listening, who knows what will happen to them?

When Gary Hart got caught on the boat with Donna Rice, he should have said, "She wasn't really a girl, she only looked like a girl. She was looking for a job at four o'clock in the morning. She was in the wrong building. She thought she was in the unemployment office. She didn't know I was a guy. She thought I was a horse, a chair, a couch. She must have thought I was a couch because she wanted to lie down next to me. She was tired. She was up late. She traveled a long distance." Now those are *bobbeh meissehs*.

28

Chicken Soup:
pronounced like it looks, and tastes

Chicken soup is one of the hallmarks of being Jewish. It has a great reputation as the all-purpose cleanser, the all-purpose medicine, the all-purpose waker-upper, the all-purpose expression of hospitality, of friendship, of neighborliness. Chicken soup, for Jews, is what a pizza, a frankfurter, and an apple pie all together are for gentiles.

Chicken soup is the expression of everything a Jew represents. It's a great expression of love, and since it is served hot also conveys warmth. The fact that it's a picker-upper made it a medicine. It was also very popular from early on because it was a great way to save money on dinner. It's heavy and fattening and poor Jews always ate chicken soup. They always had potatoes on the side and chicken soup in the plate. In the broth you add a matzo ball, which is rolled up dough, or you add a kreplach, rolled dough with chopped meat inside, or you'd have rice, or noodles, or kasha, which is buckwheat. So between the potatoes and the chicken soup, the poverty-stricken Jew on the Lower East Side in New York for thirty years was able to fill himself up for twenty cents.

Chicken soup to this day is the main item for the poor people of the world, because it's a great pasta dish, even though nobody calls it that.

The gentiles of America have gotten into pasta as the great new hip fetish food. But what is a pasta dish, anyway? It's "lokshen," which is the Yiddish word for noodles.

Many Jews felt they left chicken soup and noodles behind when they moved to the suburbs. They all decided that chicken soup was too Jewish. It wasn't hip enough, it wasn't gentile enough, and didn't have enough nutritional value. It also wasn't sexy enough. So they switched from *chicken soup* to gazpacho. From gazpacho to French onion soup, and from French onion soup to minestrone soup. From that they went to quiche, and quiche became a hot item that symbolized success. Then they moved up to Japanese fish that was never cooked and called it sushi. And after all these foods, they settled on pasta.

Now when pasta became the biggest hit in hip America, Jews didn't even know it but they were back to *chicken soup* again. Pasta is nothing but chicken noodle soup when you leave out the soup. And you leave out the chicken. If you want to eat the best pasta and the hippest pasta and the smartest pasta today, you're back to *chicken soup*. One of the most popular pastas today is angel hair pasta. If an old Jew eats it, it's called *chicken soup*. If a young Jew eats it, he feels hip by calling it angel hair pasta.

And I guarantee you, pretty soon they'll start adding water back to it to make it taste better. People do that all the time. They eat the same thing that used to be eaten, but they give it new titles and they feel like a swinger because it's a new generation. Years ago I remember that a cafeteria was a cafeteria. Now, all over America people are eating in cafeterias, but they're calling them salad bars.

A cafeteria just sounded too Jewish. It sounded like a place refugees ate in, and it sounded like a way to save money on a waiter. It also made you feel like you weren't getting anywhere in life, so they came up with a name that makes it sound more continental, and if you feel continental, then you could eat in a cafeteria. And order angel hair pasta with a matzo ball.

Chochem:
pronounced, KHOH-chem

A *chochem*, or the female *chochema*, is a possessor of wisdom, a brilliant person. It's the ultimate tribute to a scholar. But it can also be said of a shrewd man because he's so clever, or inventive. It is said with the highest respect, like "A *chochem* of the Talmud." Yet it can also be used in a negative way, to make fun of somebody. You'd say, *"Noch a chochem"*; that is, "Another scholar!" Or "Uch, this is a nuclear scientist? A brain surgeon he'll never be. A genius he's not."

You reverse the meaning so that you call someone a *chochem* when you don't want to call him a jerk. And a Jew adds a little disparaging grunt, "Uch, a *chochem!*"

When a boss is talking about his favorite employee, he calls him a *chochem*. He means, "Oh, boy, he's lucky to have this guy." But when an employee is talking about his boss and calls him a *chochem*, he's usually trying to tell you that his boss is a jerk, the biggest schmuck in the world, he could do without him.

When a father leaves his business to a son who has been working for him, he says, "Oy, this is a *chochem*." It's a compliment. When the son takes over and the business goes down the drain, you hear him say the same words, but with an opposite tone. The melody becomes different. This is a word where you have to get the melody down more than the word itself. If the word goes up on the first syllable, you're serious about calling someone a wise person. If it goes up at the end of the word, you mean to say that this supposedly brilliant scholar is really a total idiot.

The father always says the same thing about the son

31

because the son inevitably destroys the business. The son went to college and learned computer technology, he learned metaphysics, he learned marketing, research analysis, he studied demographics, psychology, he studied the population centers of America, and he brought it all down to subdivisions of levels of proprietorship on the basis of customer analysis. And as soon as he takes over the business—boom!—it loses $300 million.

The father never went to school in his life, came here as a refugee who escaped from a concentration camp, he's walking around with tattoos on his arms and somehow, no matter how much he makes, no matter how he built this little shop into a big business, the son only knows one thing: His father doesn't know what he's doing; the guy is still working from yesterday's news. The son used to say, "He's making $300 million, but if I took over the business, it would be worth $500 billion. You call this a business? You know how much money Donald Trump made this year?"

Then the father hands over the business to him and says, "Go ahead." The son asks, "Now?" He takes over the business and all of a sudden he's making $1.80. That's when the father says, "Oy, this is a *chochem*." But he's a different kind of *chochem* than before. The accent is now on the second syllable. But the son, to protect himself, never hears the intonation of the word. He says, "My father just called me a *chochem*. I know what I'm doing!"

Chozzer:
pronounced, KHA-zer

chozzer literally means "a pig," and is used to describe a piggish person. It's a guy who wants everything whether it belongs to him or not, and wants one hundred times more than he has a right to expect. Like you give someone a shirt as a gift. Instead of him accepting the shirt with a thank you, the *chozzer* says, "What, only one shirt? Can't I have at least three more?" When he exchanges the shirt for one that's twice as expensive, he expects you to pay for that, too.

When you invite a *chozzer* to a bar mitzvah, you can be sure he'll show up with twelve of his relatives. He figures he has a lot of people who have no place to go tonight, and he wants to see them, too.

When a *chozzer* sits in a restaurant and orders a chicken, he eats the whole chicken and then calls the owner over and says, "This chicken came out terrible. I deserve something else." He tries to get another main dish to replace the one he just devoured. A normal person might take a bite of something, and then call over the owner, but not the *chozzer*. He waits to finish it first and then wants his money back. The owner says, "If the chicken was no good, how come it's not on your plate? How did the chicken disappear? Was the sanitation department here to pick it up on a truck? No, you ate it!" The *chozzer* says, "Who ate it? I didn't eat the chicken. Maybe the guy next to me ate the chicken. New York is a dangerous place. People will steal anything. How should I know where the chicken went? I'm not a detective. All I know is I'm still hungry. I want something to eat."

A *chozzer* has endless *chutzpah*. There's no such thing as a *chozzer* without *chutzpah*, though you can have *chutzpah* and not be a *chozzer*.

A companion saying is, A *chozzer bleibt a chozzer* (*bleibt* is pronounced, bligh-bt).

It means that a pig always remains a pig no matter what. If a guy does something wrong to you and then does it a second time, this symbolizes the fact that he can't learn, he can't improve, and he won't change. A leopard doesn't change his spots. You can't teach an old dog new tricks. The man was a pig, he is a pig, and he'll die a pig. This man is an unchange able commodity. He stinks from the bottom up, and always will.

Chutzpah:
pronounced, KHOOTS-pah

Someone with *chutzpah* is brazen, brash, and has the gall to tell you off even when you did nothing to him. He's abusing you and making demands on you that he has no right to expect. A guy with *chutzpah* takes out a gun and shoots you in the heart and then blames you for being in the wrong place at the wrong time. If not for you, he wouldn't be charged with murder. You had the gall to drop dead after he shot you. If you hadn't done that to him, he'd be a man without problems.

A guy crashes a wedding and is caught and thrown out. He asks, "What are you doing?" The groom says, "You don't belong here. Nobody invited you." The guy with *chutzpah* figures that he would never have rented the suit if the groom wasn't getting married, so he sends him the bill for it.

Di Emmeseh Schoireh:
pronounced, deh EM-messeh SKOY-reh

*T*his means "the ultimate truth, the real thing, the best you can find." It is usually accompanied by a shortness of breath. When a Jew looks at a girl who is stunning, he says, "Ooh, this is the *emmeseh!*" It's when you're out of control because something is so great. *Emmeseh* means the ultimate, but it doesn't have to be sex. It could be a car, a pair of shoes, a pastrami sandwich. Whatever is the best.

Whenever you get something for wholesale, it becomes *di emmeseh schoireh.* If you got it at cost, it becomes *di richtik schoireh.* That's one step better than *di emmeseh schoireh.* This is the real real McCoy, and there's never been another McCoy like it.

Draykop:
pronounced, DRAY-kop, or DRAY-kawp

A *draykop* is someone who talks about nothing and gives you a headache. It's everybody's sister-in-law or brother-in-law. It's a scatterbrain, but more than that, it's a chatterer. Someone whose conversation is pointless and hopeless and endless. It's someone who keeps talking even though the conversation is going nowhere because the greatest fear in their life is to keep quiet.

They can't keep quiet. *Draykops* are people with the least to say and take the longest to say it.

The literal meaning of a *draykop* is "turn-head," someone who's head is turned from talking so much, or who turns your head around from listening to them. They can't say hello without trying to impress you about where they're going, what they're doing, and they'll include fifty *bobbeh meissehs* in two minutes.

You say hello to a *draykop* and he tells you he's a producer and he's making three pictures this week. He asks, "Did you see my last four movies?" "No," you tell him, "I never saw them." He says, "I don't know how you missed them." You missed them because he never made a movie in his life.

A *bobbeh meisseh* will tell you he bought the Empire State Building. A *draykop* thinks he actually did. Not only that, but a *draykop* actually brings his furniture into the lobby because he thinks it belongs there.

A *draykop* could be a con man, but he's more of a blowhard. A *draykop* lives in his own fantasy world. He dresses up to go to his own wedding without a girl. He doesn't even have a girlfriend. He goes places he doesn't belong and thinks he's been invited. He's the ultimate gate crasher. He thinks he's on his way to the White House to advise the president.

A *draykop* always drops names and he convinces himself he actually met these people. He'll tell you he went fishing with George Bush on Thursday. He says, "I don't like how the disarmament conference is going. I spoke to him about it last night, but I didn't get anywhere with him." "Why not?" "The television was on and it was playing too loud. But I'm going back." "Why?" "He's dying to see me again." "Did you talk about anything else?" "The missile crisis." "But there hasn't been any missile crisis." "No wonder we didn't settle it. Oh, boy. Am I glad you told me. That's why nothing worked out."

A *draykop* likes to go into details of conversations he never had, about things that never happened, and he has solutions to problems he never heard about. And before you know it, he's involved with every problem in the world. He solved three-quarters of them. The rest he's working on, and yet he never left his house. He's still trying to save up enough money to make a phone call.

He's also a financial genius; he's figured out a way to save the world. The first thing you do, he says, is eliminate trees. Or curbs. Or shoelaces. He always has fantastic fantasies that will straighten out everything. And nothing has to make sense. It only has to make sense in his own mind.

He keeps talking and his head keeps swelling and he doesn't care if you're listening or not. By the time he's finished, he feels so important he doesn't need you altogether. He's already impressed with himself and he leaves.

Du Zol Nicht Vissen Frum Tsores:
pronounced, doo zohl nikht viss-en froom TZOHR-ehs

I t means, "You should never know from human misery, from sorrow, or from agony." *Tsores* is the equivalent of troubles. It's an all-inclusive word that deals with problems or tragedies or negative emotions of any kind. And naturally the reverse of it is, you should only know from happiness. To a Jewish mother, they don't want you to know from *tsores*. Only happiness. They are like watchdogs against troubles.

If a Jewish mother sees you sitting and thinking, she gets worried. Every Jewish mother is the same. They interrupt you right away because it looks dangerous. They say, "What are you thinking about? You're thinking too hard." You say, "I'm just trying to figure something out."

"What are you thinking? Be happy, be comfortable, why do you have to take life so seriously?"

"I'm not taking it seriously. I happen to have a problem. I have to solve it."

"Solve problems! What do you have to worry about problems? A man like you has everything he wants in life. You're healthy, you're making a living, you have to worry about problems? Forget about the problem."

"But the problem is, I have a house. I have to put it up."

"Wha-a-t up? Up is not important. A house is a house. You never saw a house before?"

"But don't you have to figure out how to build it?"

"What build? There are builders that build it as fast as you. Why are you getting involved?"

My mother was like that, too. She never wanted me to even think of something. Once I'm thinking, I'm too quiet. Quiet to them means a problem. "What's bothering you?" "Nothing's bothering me. I'm just quiet." "You're not just quiet. I can tell there's something on your mind. When you get quiet, you start to think, when you start to think, you get depressed. Where do you think ulcers come from? Forget about it." "But I've got nothing to forget about." "Then forget about nothing. Go out and enjoy yourself."

Er Zol Vaksen Vi a Tsibeleh, Mit Dem Kop in Drerd!:

pronounced, ehr zohl VAHK-sen vee ah TSIB-el-eh, mitt dem KOHP in DRAYRD

"He should grow like an onion with his head in the ground" is the direct translation. What it means is, He should drop dead. Head first.

He shouldn't even take a chance that his feet should go first because then he might realize where he's going and get out in time. But if he goes head first, then he can't change his mind. He's already buried before he can think it over. He's wiped out before he knew what hit him. When you wish this, then you believe the guy doesn't deserve a conversation or the courtesy to yell for help—he can't yell for help because his head's in the ground already.

One who gets this fate wished upon him is the worst kind of person. He could have done anything. He could have evicted your mother from her apartment. He could have called your sister a whore. He could have loaned you nine dollars and not had the decency to stop hounding you about it, starting five minutes after he loaned it to you.

Or you see someone that you loaned nine dollars to sitting in a delicatessen with soup in front of him. Just as he's about to start, you take the plate from under his mouth and tell him, "What right do you have to live so good when you owe me money?" And then you tell him you wish he'd grow like an onion with his head in the ground.

You might also say this to a woman you were making love to and at the height of your excitement, she says, "Excuse me, I want to get a chicken sandwich."

39

You're on the highway in the mountains at night and you get a flat tire. There's only one other car on the road. You wave the guy down. He stops and asks, "What's the matter?" You tell him you have a flat tire. He says, "I see, but I'm looking for directions for a hotel. Do you know how to get there?" You say you do and give him the directions. He gets back in his car, and you say, "But what about my flat tire?" He says, "I have no time for your flat tire, I have to find my hotel." And he drives off. If ever a guy should grow like an onion with his head in the ground, that's him.

Farbissener:
pronounced, far-BISS-in-er

Any woman with a sister-in-law who has more money than she does will most definitely be a *farbisseneh*. A *farbissener*, or female *farbisseneh*, is an embittered person, someone who is sour about anything and everything.

Any comedian who learns that another comedian got paid more for the same show is a *farbissener*. He's jealous and envious and it's killing him. Any guy who sees the guy across the street has two more customers than he does is also a *farbissener*.

A *farbissener* is always irritable. He's the guy who feels the world should send him checks for nothing. That he should not have to get up in the morning to go to work. There has never been a bus that has arrived on time for a *farbissener*. A *farbissener* is someone that feels you owe him something, but doesn't know what, and wants it right away, but he doesn't know why. Even if he got it, he still wouldn't be happy. Because then he couldn't complain. If a *farbissener* can't complain, he might drop dead on the spot.

Fargess:
pronounced, far-GESS

his literally means forgot. It is an attitude and you often hear it in a sarcastic phrase, like "With all your learning put together, you don't know half of what I forgot already." Or "What I forgot is more than you already learned in your whole life." This means that you are trying to sound like you have the wisdom of the ages but you're sounding pretentious and you're basically a person who is simple or naive or stupid or untrained or unlearned or unsuited or unknowledgeable or ignorant or all of those things combined.

When someone wants to tell you he's smarter than you, knows something more about a subject, wasn't born yesterday, in English he could say, "I've been around the block more than once. I know this and don't you compare yourself to me. I've got a lot of mileage in this department. I've been through this backwards and forwards. So who you bullshitting, mister?"

A salesman is trying to sell you a shirt. He's pressuring you about how great the shirt is. You tell him you don't think the shirt is so hot. In fact, you think it stinks. He gets pushy.

41

You say, "Look, take it easy. With all your learning about shirts, you should only know as much as I've forgotten about shirts."

Fargess is often used by the guy who knows nothing about a certain field. When he can't give you factual information, he tells you you'll never know half as much as he's forgotten. It's a saying common in political discussions. Two guys are arguing about Russia and neither one has any way to prove his point. So they start using insults to try to dominate the conversation.

One guy says, "You could study for a hundred years and still not know what I know on this subject." The other guy says, "What! Are you telling me that the czar of Russia was always a wonderful person? He was the worst bastard that ever lived."

"Look, what I forgot about the czar of Russia is ten times more than you ever learned about him."

"Are you kidding? The czar of Russia is my field."

It's an argument nobody can prove. Like the one in which one guy says, "That's a beautiful girl." His friend says, "That's not a beautiful girl. You're going to tell me about beautiful girls?"

The first guy says, "Oh, yeah? What do you know about beautiful girls?"

And when the other guy is stuck for an answer, he comes out with, "You'll never know what I forget even." To him, that wins the argument once and for all.

Farputst:
pronounced, far-PUTST

When someone gets all dolled up, all decorated, dressed to kill, someone else says, "Look how *farputst!*" A husband surprises a wife by putting on a clean shirt with cuff links attached to it, and wearing a tie that he usually saves only for bar mitzvahs and weddings. Immediately the wife is wondering if he's got something going on the side. She says, "So, where are you going so *farputst?*"

And if he says, "Oh, nowhere," then he's in trouble.

A woman is going to have a date with "Mr. Right," and so she goes and buys an expensive dress, spends all day in the beauty parlor, and has her special manicurist work a double shift on her fingers. When she's finally ready to go out, with every hair in place and the eye shadow just perfect, a friend says, "You look so *farputst*, I didn't recognize you." The woman might take this as a compliment, but it's really an insult, because this means that normally she looks like she just woke up.

Feh:
pronounced, fehh!

Feh is the shortest, most efficient way in the Yiddish language to say something stinks. *Feh* is the most undiplomatic way and the clearest and fastest way to say, "Boy, does that smell!" You could say it about everything from a leftover herring to an opera.

Ordinarily, a diplomatic person would say, "I don't think it's so great." A more honest person would say, "I'm sorry, I don't like it *that* much." But an honest Jew says the same thing when something it not so hot. *"Feh!"*

Feh is something you say to a friend about another guy. If someone is walking around with a shirt that you can't stand, and he asks your opinion of it, you're not going to tell him it looks like nothing. You just tell him, "I don't think it looks that great." But when you and your friend are discussing what someone else is wearing, the conversation goes, "You know that guy's shirt?" "Yeah?" *"Feh!"*

It's something you'd never say to a guy's face unless you want to get rapped in the mouth. Or the guy is three feet tall and you're six-foot-eight, but if he's six-foot-eight and you're three feet tall you'd never say *"Feh!"* about anything he might take as personal.

Feh is the word that every mother-in-law has about her daughter-in-law for the rest of her life wherever she lives. This is the ultimate word whenever you're talking to somebody who just turned the other way.

When someone shows you his grandchild's picture, the reaction is usually predictable. You say, "I never saw such a beautiful baby." What you're really thinking is *"Feh!" Feh* means the kid looks like nothing, but how could I tell this guy that I just saw the ugliest baby in my life?

A woman is going with a guy who has lavished her with furs and jewels. He's such a wonderful person. He's tops. Then comes the stock market crash, and he goes from being a millionaire to a guy who doesn't even have change for the bus. Now when he calls, she doesn't answer. When she sees him on the street, she looks the other way. Before, he was marvelous. Now what is he? He's *"feh!"*

It's late and you drop by a girl's apartment for a visit. As things heat up a little you tell her, "I can't get over you. You're the most magnificent thing that ever happened." In your own mind, you're saying, "Better than nothing. This is the best I could get. It's 4:00 in the morning. What do you expect?" But by 4:15, when you take a look at the girl, and your honest opinion becomes clear, it is summed up in one word that you're thinking. That word is: *"Feh."* *Feh* goes together with, How can I get a cab as fast as possible?

Only later do you learn that she had the same word in mind about you. You thought it was your good luck that a cab showed up so fast, but what you didn't know was that she had called for it.

Frum Dein Moil Tzu Gott's Erin:
pronounced, froom DINE moyle tsoo GOTT'S err-in

It literally means, "From your mouth to God's ears." It should only happen, whatever it is you're hoping for. God should only be listening. It comes when you want to give somebody a compliment. You say, "I see you're losing weight." The guy knows he's not really losing weight. He says, *"Frum dein moil tzu Gott's erin."* It should only be half as true as you're imagining it.

"All your ambitions in life should come true" is another way of interpreting it. God should only be listening to the words you just said because I know it's a longshot, I haven't got a chance, but if there's any possibility it requires God's help, so I hope he's hearing about it.

You hear this phrase a lot regarding hopes for children. Your son is three-and-a-half years old, but already the future is clear to his uncle. He tells you, "This is the one that's going to become a doctor." And that's when you say, "Frum dein moit tzu Gott's erin."

Fumfer:
pronounced, FOOM-fehr

This is someone who can't talk straight, who talks through his nose, or who just plain double-talks. A guy who's not articulate, whose words are not coming out clearly. His words are all botched up in his throat, bungled up, and he has to try to rearrange them. His tongue is tied in his mouth and his foot is in-between and he's dying to get the words right, but he just can't. It could be that he has some kind of mental block about the words, or he's nervous, or he's lying and can't extract the words the way he had planned.

A guy decides that he's going to see his boss about a raise. He goes into the office, clears his throat, and begins to *fumfer*. He had his mind made up, everything was set, his shirt is pressed, his lips are open, everything is perfect except that the words won't come out right. And all you hear are incoherent noises. He's nervous, he's in a panic, he's *fumfering*.

You catch a pickpocket with his hand on your wallet.

You yell, "Hey, what's your hand doing in my pocket?" The thief is in a panic and talks so fast that he doesn't make any sense: "I thought it was my pocket. You're so close to me. How should I know it was your pocket? There's a lot of pockets on this bus. I'm supposed to know which one's mine?" He chokes and gargles like he's got a piece of bagel caught in his throat. That's called a *fumfer*.

Gantseh Megillah:
pronounced, GONT-seh meh-GILL-ah

It means to make a big deal or a major issue out of nothing.
Someone asks, "What time is it?" And instead of simply answering the question, the other guy tells you where he bought his watch, how much it cost, how many watches he's got like that, and what time it is all over the world. He gives you the time in Africa, in Poland, in Turkey. Then he tells you the meaning of time, why time isn't important, and why you should never be in a hurry. And people should never ask the time because if you're only worried about time you'll get an ulcer. And you never do find out what time it is. He gives you a *gantseh megillah*.

When you ask him one question, he reads you thirty pages of the *Haftorah*. You ask him, "Where's Third Street?" Instead of telling you where it is, he tells you what's wrong with the neighborhood, how long it took to build, and why the fire escapes are a health hazard.

If you ask, "How do you like this jacket?" instead of

giving his opinion of the jacket, he gives you a list of tailors all over the country where you can get a better one and tells you how you can get it cheaper from a factory in Philadelphia or Bangkok. You're not asking him about jackets all over the world. You're asking him if your jacket is a nice jacket.

This doesn't faze him. He wants to take you home and show you how many jackets he's got that are nicer than yours. A *gantseh megilla* for one little jacket.

Gefilte Fish:
IIIIIIIIIIIIIIIIIIIIIIIIIIIIIIIIIIIIIIIIIIIIIIIIIIIII
pronounced, geh-FILL-teh fish. And CHRAINE, pronounced like crane, but with the gutteral "kh" for the "c"

I would say that the most popular Jewish dish, the most traditional Jewish dish is *gefilte fish*. *Gefilte fish* was originated by Jews in Eastern Europe. Since they couldn't afford one whole fish, they would grind up pieces of leftover fish and pack it together. It was a new fish: *Gefilte fish*, *gefilte* meaning, in Yiddish, "stuffed."

Chraine means "horseradish" in Yiddish, and was the favorite condiment put on *gefilte fish* to give it a sharper taste. It's a bitter taste, and it was probably added to kill the taste of the original stuffed fish. *Chraine* contributes to giving a Jew heartburn, and Jews and heartburn go together. You almost never see a gentile that says to you, "I got heartburn." Every second Jew has heartburn. And every time you say hello to a Jew, he's got Rolaids, he's got Maalox, he's got pills. You get a medicine chest whenever you talk to a Jew. Gentiles carry pocketbooks with combs and lipstick. Jews carry those items, too, but most of their pocketbooks are filled with medicines.

Even the healthiest Jews have medicines and pills. You would think it's only a sick person who has them, who's ninety-seven years old and in a wheelchair and who was told to take a pill every three minutes. The healthiest Jew, I don't care if he's nine years old, he already has Rolaids. He's got toys and Rolaids, because already he has an upset stomach. When the gentile is playing ball, the Jew is taking pills.

When I play a date at a gentile club and I get a head-ache—I'm not given to headaches, but once in a while I get a headache—I could walk around the area a whole day and not find a single person with aspirin. But when I used to walk into Grossinger's and say I have a headache, five thousand yentas were opening pillboxes.

They got pills for bigger headaches and for smaller head-aches. They ask "You have a migraine?" Now they all become doctors. "You have a strong migraine or a weak migraine? Because I only have for a weak migraine. Shirley has for a strong migraine. You want a number three? I got a number three. How long you got it?" Now they become experts. "You got it for an hour and a quarter? I got a white pill, I got a green one for an hour and a half. I got this one for three hours. I got something else for nine hours."

Then they say, "I got one for walking. Are you going to be sitting or are you going to be dancing? If you're dancing I got a dancing pill. Are you going to be dancing fast or slow? I got a fast-dance pill and a slow-dance pill. Are you going to walk after you dance? Or are you going to lie down for an hour? I got for lying down or for standing up."

They've got every pill you could imagine. "Don't take this before you eat. Only eat a little before you take that. And

49

drink all the water you can. Seltzer would be even better. But if you got no seltzer, plain soda. And watch out! Not too much. And take one every three hours unless you get a little nauseated. Then take one every four hours. You'll find that the pill dries up your throat. This is for a dry throat after the pill. This is for the sore throat before the pill. Then as you're going home, you'll notice that when you see the house you get a little dizzy. I got a dizzy pill after the dry one."

They've got something for every kind of headache and every kind of stomach condition, and there's no disease you could have that they don't have a pill for. And then they always have the addresses of the best doctors in the field. "Don't go to him for the stomach. I got a better guy. Your guy is okay for the upper stomach, he'd be perfect. But you got a lower stomach. Forget about it, he'll kill you. He doesn't know anything about a lower stomach. What else? You got the abdomen? On which side? This side? I got a doctor for this side that is fantastic. He's a left-side doctor. You can't top him."

They've got addresses on top of addresses, medical advice on top of medical advice, pills on top of pills. And it all started with *gefilte fish.*

Gehakteh Leber:
pronounced, geh-HAK-teh LEE-ber

This is chopped liver, and Jews are always involved with eating chopped liver. Chopped liver has been such an essential part of the past of Jewish people that any time someone is stuck for something to say he compares it to chopped liver.

You see a beautiful girl, and your friend says, "What a stunning girl." You say, "So what did you think she was, chopped liver?"

Someone asks, "Are you making a living?" The other person says, "What am I, chopped liver?"

A woman asks, "Where are you going?" The guy says, "To Pittsburgh." She says, "Are you taking me?" He says, "No." She says, "No? What am I, chopped liver?" Any time someone feels left out, they say, "What am I, chopped liver?"

You come back from Pittsburgh and she asks, "How come you didn't wait for me?" You tell her, "I didn't know you were there." She replies, "What am I, chopped liver?" Jews are wondering about chopped liver all the time.

A man in a restaurant orders chopped liver, and the waiter tells him he has no chopped liver. The man asks, "Why haven't you got any chopped liver?" The waiter says, "Look, it happens I don't have any more chopped liver."

"Why?"

"Because I don't have any."

"You had chopped liver for the other guy over there. How come you have no chopped liver for me? What am I, chopped liver?"

"What is he, chopped liver? He happened to get the last piece of chopped liver."

51

Chopped liver is always used as an excuse to complain about everything. Whenever somebody wants something he can't get, he asks about chopped liver.

If a guy is standing on line in a bank and he sees somebody push ahead of him, right away he says, "Mister, where are you going? Don't you see I'm standing here? What am I, chopped liver?"

Chopped liver, like *chicken soup* and *gefilte fish,* has always been a cheap item; everybody who couldn't afford almost any-thing else at least could afford chopped liver. And anyone who didn't have a friend in the world and had no place to go always knew the one thing he could depend on was chopped liver.

Chopped liver is the ultimate argument, too. Any time somebody wants to make a fool out of someone, he asks about chopped liver. Chopped liver means "no matter what you said, it's stupid." Because if you compare it to chopped liver, you're proving to the person that he's an idiot, and without calling him names. If you call him names, you're crude, but if you compare anything to chopped liver, then you think of yourself as being able to show a brilliant example.

So when somebody can't think of another example or comparison because he has no intelligence, the first thing he compares it to is chopped liver. If he had any intelligence, he would pick something else. A piece of fish, a slice of cake, a glass of tea. A lot of people can't even think of a simple thing like raisins or toast. They can't even think of a tomato. But chopped liver is the ultimate haven for anyone whose mind has completely stopped working.

Someone asks, "Do you think Russia should have invaded Afghanistan?" His friend says, "Positively not." "Why not?" "Afghanistan has the right to be completely independent just like any other country. What do you think it is, chopped liver?"

Countries are compared to chopped liver, women are compared to chopped liver, shirts are compared to chopped liver. It's the only word in the world that everything is compared to. You never have to worry about saying it out of place. It's always in place.

Geshmak:
pronounced, geh-SHMOK

It means savory, delicious, a fabulous taste. It's directly related to observations of food, but it can also have meaning for other things. You could say it about beauty or people. Like "She's a sweet person, a wonderful person." Or "He's a *geshmakteh mensh.*" *Geshmak* in a broad sense means, "Ooh, you can't top it when it comes to flavor."

You could say it when a guy gets rich. "Ooh, *geshmak.*" That means, "Thank God. You got the right taste now." This is how sweet it is. And it could be used just as much about a fabulous feeling.

It can also be used with feelings of temptation, or lustful yearnings. You'd like to be so close to feel the flavor of another person, as if you'd like to taste the other person. For a man, he's dying for a girl he can't get. "Ooh, is this *geshmak!*" This means, "What a heavenly experience that would be."

But it began with food. "Boy, look at this corned beef

53

sandwich! My God! This comes in a big bulky size. You could choke a horse with it. It looked *geshmak.*"

You take a bit. "Mmmm. It is *geshmak!*"

Gib Mir Nit Kain Einoreh!:
pronounced, gib MEER nit kine-a-HAW-reh

"Don't give me the canary" is the literal translation of this saying, but its interpretation is "Don't give me the evil eye."

Jews have always been superstitious and they think of an evil eye as a curse. For centuries, Jews have been warding off curses and inflicting them. An example of this exchange would be when someone recognizes how well you're doing, he somehow comes up with the idea that because of his jealousy and envy he can influence the supernatural to send bad luck your way.

If you're doing well, or your son's doing well, you don't want anyone to talk or think about it. Jews think that this might ruin them. They imagine God is up there waiting for somebody to mention it and then who knows what can happen. That's why when you ask a Jew how much money he makes a week, he can't tell you because it would be a *Gib mir nit kain einoreh.* He's allowed to admit that he's doing well, but he's not allowed to admit that he's doing *too* well. He can't give specifics.

Meanwhile, Jews will show you their boats, their cars, they'll spend the whole day showing you pictures, they won't leave out one thing that they own from the conversation, they'll show you *all* the things that are worth millions, but if you ask them if they got money, they don't. They don't want to have a *kain einoreh!* As if they have no wealth at all. But they just happen to own the whole world. It's a coincidence.

No Jew will ever say he's rich. If you ask him, he'll say he's comfortable. *Rich* will give him a *kain einoreh*. He'll say "I own Spain. I own Portugal. I own Africa. I own it all, it's all mine. And everything you see all over the world is under my name." When you ask, "Are you making a living?" and he says, "Not right now. Right now it's a little rough. I owe a lot of money," he's afraid of the evil eye. He's concerned that somebody somewhere will take what he has away from him. He doesn't know how. Like if God finds out he has it, he'll ask for it back. God doesn't mind if you use it, but if you admit you own it, you're in for a lot of trouble.

Goy:
pronounced, like "Roy"

Any gentile is called a *goy*. Plural is *goyim*. It has nothing to do with the quality or character of a person. It is strictly an identifying term. It can be used derisively, however, by Jews as well as by gentiles when gentiles want to put themselves down, or want to poke fun at themselves when they think they've done or said something stupid. They'll refer to themselves as having "a *goyishe kop*." A gentile head. "What can you do? I've got a *goyishe kop*."

55

Jews were always considered by gentiles to be somehow either crooked or manipulating or shrewd or clever or brilliant. They always felt that Jewish brain power is outstanding in some special way. Jews and brains always seemed to go together in the minds of gentiles, and even in the minds of Jews. Maybe both sides have convinced themselves that the Jew is gifted in brain power to a greater extent than the gentile. Just like whites always thought they were brighter than blacks, or men always thought they were smarter than women, or that blacks have greater physical or sexual prowess than whites. People actually buy these stories.

When a Jew wants to hire a mechanic, it will always be a gentile, because the belief is that gentiles work better manually than Jews. When a Jew wants to hire an accountant, though, it's always a Jew. And that goes for gentiles as well. You never see a gentile looking for a gentile doctor or lawyer, or dentist. Everybody wants a Jew to fix his arm, to work on his divorce, or to do his root canal.

All of them somehow feel that this is the expertise of the Jew. That if you need the brightest guy possible, find a Jew. Also for gentiles, if you want the crookedest guy possible, find a Jew.

But in reality there's nobody brighter than anybody else or more crooked than anybody else. But the fact is that the Jews have had to use their ingenuity more than many others. If I'm persecuted and I'm denied access to everything in the world, if I'm alienated and divided and separated from everything that society has to offer, I have to find a way to succeed. So I have to work ten times as hard. It's compensating for what you don't have, or what's not been simply handed to you.

It's like the blind man who hears better than you because he's listening harder. And so has it been for the Jew in history.

56

If you can't make a deal one way, you've got to find another way. Your mind has to work better because you're more challenged. Necessity is the mother of invention, and before you know it you're thinking harder than the other guy because he's already there, and he already has it, and you're fighting to get there and get it, too. A prisoner finds an escape route that a free person would never think of. He has to find a way to open a door. All of a sudden, he seems ten times brighter than the warden. He's more creative because he has no choice and he's determined.

Jews, as it happened, went on to excel in many areas of the mind. When people wanted a great brain, they'd look to Einstein in physics, or Freud in psychiatry, or Kissinger in diplomacy. I even include my own accountant, whose name is Teitelbaum.

Haimish:
pronounced, HAME-ish

aimish means homey, warm, cuddly. It's usually used in the sense of "He's a *haimisheh* person." It is somebody sweet, natural, unpretentious, kind, gentle, likeable. Somebody you feel comfortable to be with. If *haimish* was furniture, you could call it cozy for the apartment. A *haimisheh* person is not trying to prove a point and is not involved in status symbols. It's a real sweetheart of a person.

But it could also be used in the opposite way. If someone is trying to fix up a girl with a blind date, and the girl asks,

"How does he look?" and she's told, "He's got a nice personality," or "He's brilliant," that's always followed by "He's very *haimish.*" Immediately you know he doesn't look so hot.

Whenever I heard, "*Oy,* she's such a *haimisheh maedel*"—such a down-to-earth girl—you knew she was a social worker, that she wore glasses, her nose was a little crooked, and her legs were never too straight, and that she was humble. She was humble because she couldn't help being humble. You're always humble if nobody's talking to you.

It's no accident that stunning girls always look like they don't need a friend. It's a supply-and-demand market. The more stunning the person, the less they need anyone. It's like a millionaire. What does he need you for? Everybody's looking at him.

Millionaires and pretty girls have one common quality—arrogance. If there are ten gorgeous girls at a party, and one other girl is short and fat and has a moustache, nobody will be trying to talk to her. So she has to try every trick in the world to get your attention. While the others are trying every trick in the world to lose your attention. The gorgeous girls have a crowd waiting on line to talk to them. So the girl with the moustache has to be very friendly; and that's why she's called *haimish.* Stunning girls are very seldom called *haimish.* They're just called stunning.

When a pretty girl says hello to you, you say, "Oh, she's such a sweet, charming lady." You're so taken with her because you never expected her to answer you. It's the same thing with a star. If Frank Sinatra says, "Hello," the whole country gets excited. "Look what a friendly person he is, he said, 'Hello'!" He opened the door and you said hello to him. He has to answer you. Who was he going to talk to, the wall?

Stars always act like they live in another world, apart

from the rest of the people. That's because people treat them that way. They look at a star as if he's not really human, like he's a painting. And pretty soon he starts to walk around feeling and acting like he's made out of some different kind of material.

Somehow when you see a star even going to the men's room, you can't believe it. Subconsciously, people think that stars actually don't go to the toilet. And if they do, they don't really use it—they just stand around watching other people.

You can't really call that *haimish* just because he does something that seems human. A *haimisheh* person is not impressed with who he is himself. He doesn't judge you or himself by status symbols. If he has $100 million he's comfortable riding in a Chevy as much as a Rolls Royce. A *haimisheh* guy doesn't have to have to buy a thirty-foot boat. He doesn't have to have a fake library in his house with books without pages just to try to prove to you how brilliant he is.

A *haimisheh* person judges you by your character, not your money, by your mind, not your station in life. If he says hello to Rockefeller and Rockefeller says something stupid, he'll walk away from him.

Harry Truman, for example, had the appearance of being *haimish*, and Franklin Roosevelt did not. There was something about Roosevelt that was so grandiose and presidential that people felt reverent as soon as they saw him. You could never imagine being casual with Roosevelt and saying something like "Come here, Frank, I want to talk to you." He seemed the type of guy who, if you called him *haimish*, would punch you in the mouth.

Harry Truman was accessible and natural. He was the vice-president first but he looked and sounded like he never really became the president. He had the job, but he didn't really notice. He looked like he knew how to handle it and did so because he was responsible for it, but he never seemed to wear the mantle of high office.

Every time Truman spoke he sounded like he really didn't think anybody was listening. When Roosevelt talked, he sounded like the whole world was listening and that every word counted. Truman talked like you had just woken him up at 4:00 in the morning and he just happened to tell you what he thought of you before he went back to sleep. He didn't act like he had to depend on your vote. This is what he has to tell you. If you want to listen, it's up to you.

Harry Truman even dressed like he never thought he was president. He never had a sleek look like a special designer came to fix him up. Everything he wore seemed like his hat, which always looked flat on his head, and with the brim pushed back. His glasses looked like he bought them in a flea market. His shirt looked like he got a bargain on it. The tie looked like it was outdated by forty years. You knew just by looking at him that he wasn't in it for the show. You knew he wasn't in it for the power, either, and that he was defiitely *haimish*.

Hak Mir Nit Kain Tsheinik:
IIIIIIIIIIIIIIIIIIIIIIIIIIIIIIIIIIIIIIIIIIIIIIIIIIIIIIIIIIIIIIIIIIIIIIIIIIIIIIIIIIIIIIIIIIIIIIIIIIIIIIIIIIIIIIIIIIIII
pronounced, HOCK meer nit kane CHIN-eek

The literal translation is "Don't bang on the tea kettle." It means, "Stop knocking so much, stop making so much noise"—in other words, "Stop bothering me!"

When a person says something, you listen. When he says it a second time, you try to be polite. By the *third* time, you're nauseated from it already. *Hak mir nit kain tsheinik* is like when a tea kettle is clopping and perking and jerking and jumping and bopping before the tea's out. It's somebody talking so much that he creates a clamoring in your head. That's when you say, "Stop banging like a tea kettle! All right already, I've heard it too many times!"

I'm sure that every married man at one time or another has thought about his wife and said to himself, "Stop banging on the tea kettle already!" It's usually when she's nagging him, asking for the same thing over and over again. She says, "Put on your pajamas." You say, "I'm putting on my pajamas." She says, "What's taking you so long to put on your pajamas? Don't you have your pajamas on yet?" And when your pajamas are on, she might go to another subject: "Did you close the window?" You tell her, "I closed it." She says, "You mean you closed it already? You closed the window?" You repeat, "I closed it." She says, "It doesn't feel closed. You should close it again."

She reminds you of something three hundred times. You're reading the paper and the next thing you hear is, "Listen, I think it's a good idea for you to call your daughter."

"That's good, thank you. I think I'll call her."

"Did you call her yet?"

"I didn't get a chance yet."

"What's taking you so long?"

"I haven't put the paper down yet."

"How long does it take you to put a paper down?"

"Okay! I'm putting the paper down."

"So how come it's still in your hands?"

"I'm dropping it from my hands now."

"Then leave it and call."

61

"All right, I'll call."

"So did you call yet?"

"I'm calling right now."

"But I noticed you're still not on the phone."

"I am on the phone."

"So how come I don't hear you talking?"

And finally when you can't take it anymore, you scream, "Stop banging so much on the tea kettle!"

A person that elicits such a response is talking past the point that serves a purpose. She can't make her point often enough. You got the point a week ago and she's still explaining it. And you thank God you can put a stop to it: *"Hak mir nit kain tsheinik!"*

Handle:
pronounced, HON-dle

To *handle* is to bargain, to negotiate, or to work out a deal. A Jew never considers himself Jewish if he doesn't know how to *handle*. One way a Jew proves his intelligence is by being a good *handler*. If a Jew ever pays the price that anybody ever asked for, the whole family will look at him like he's an idiot.

When a Jew comes home from buying something, there are always two questions: "What did they ask?" and "What did you pay?" If the storekeeper asked $300 and you paid $299 or anything close to $300, you are considered stupid because the most you should have paid for a $300 item was $80.

A Jew can't stand for you to make a profit on him. A

Jew knows that he should never buy anything, unless it's at cost. Or better yet, *below* cost. That's why every Jewish store owner, no matter how well he's doing, always has a Going Out of Business Sale. A sale is an offshoot of *handling*. It makes the buyer think he's getting an item cheap. A Jewish store-keeper always knows that you're not going to buy anything unless he was going out of business and was desperate to sell his goods at a bargain. So a Jewish storekeeper always has all kinds of sales and always stays in business.

A gentile only has a Christmas Sale or a George Washington Sale. But Jewish store owners in Miami Beach have sales every day that no one has ever heard of before. There's an Early Bird Sale, an After Dinner Sale, a Late Lunch Sale, and there's the Going Out of Business Sale, the I Already Went Out of Business Sale, and the Store Has Never Been in Business Sale.

And all of a sudden there are different percentages that you get off an item. First it's 20 percent off, then it's 50 percent, then it's 100 percent. Then 200 percent! There never seems to be any percentage too high.

Pretty soon you feel like you're paying nothing for it and that if you buy this suit at this ridiculously low price you might get arrested for robbery.

The store owner says, "All clothes must go at a loss! I'm selling out! I'm going out of business!" Everything must go at a tremendous loss and he doesn't care what he gets for it. He says he's losing money on every sale! So how come he's bring-ing in more clothes before the sale ends? Somehow the store is packed with clothes and buyers on the last day of the sale when it's supposed to be losing a fortune.

Jews never feel cheap by *handling*; it's a tradition to *handle*. There is no such thing as a one-price store among Jews, and the price is whatever the storekeeper feels you the consumer can afford. If you come in with a pressed pair of pants, the suit he is selling you is $150. If you have holes in your shoes, and you look *tsharget,* like you were falling apart, the same suit is all of a sudden $12. The price is always based on your appearance.

The only time a Jew knows he can't *handle* is when gentiles run the store. When he goes to Macy's, he sees a sign that has a price and he knows he can't argue with that sign. But as soon as he goes back to a Jewish store in his old neighborhood, no matter what the sign says, he knows it doesn't count. It's just a price written there. It is a starting price. The sign is the beginning of trying to work out a negotiated settlement.

A customer and the storekeeper always argue. Sometimes the customer took twelve trips. The customer says, "That's it, that's the most I'll pay, I'm walking out!" The storekeeper says, "If you're walking out, the hell with it! I'm not going a penny lower!" Then it becomes a contest on who will bend first.

The customer starts to walk out and that's really when the negotiations start heating up, because the storekeeper fast sees how far the customer is going to walk. The customer wants to see if the storekeeper calls him before he takes another step. So he starts walking very slowly. You never saw anybody walk so slowly out of a store. And the storekeeper is watching every step he takes.

The smart shopper knows the cards are in his hands. But suddenly the smart storekeeper says, "Wait! This suit isn't even mine. I'm not even allowed to sell it. I was holding it for my uncle on my wife's side. It's on hold. It won't be here if you come back. If you buy it now, I can give it to you." So the buyer is in a pickle, and has to make a decision about the suit and the uncle, too.

64

Then there are always certain items in the back room of the store that are saved for special customers. There are secret shirts in private stock that are never shown to the average customer. This makes the better customer feel special. That customer's greatest fear is that he will be taken off the special list and never get into the back room.

So now you can claim that you got a shirt that nobody else got. And you got it for a price nobody else got, either. Which was higher. But you are happy. You got a special deal. But you were really *handled*. It works both ways.

Ich Hob Zol in Bod:
|||||||||||||||||||||||||||||||||||||||||||||||||||||||||||||||||||||||||||||||||||||||
pronounced, ich HAWB zohl in BOHD

his literally translates as "I have you in the bath," or "I hope you sink like a ship." Either way, it's a wish that someone should disappear from your life. It means that he should be drowning by Thursday. And let him drown in the bathtub. And a bathtub is relating him to obscurity. "You should wallow in water all by yourself!" Or "You should lay there like a dead horse." These are some of the curses that are offshoots of *Ich hob zol in bod*.

It means "get lost." The man is nothing. He's a dead issue. His opinion is worthless. As far as I'm concerned, he belongs in the toilet. Or he shouldn't get out of the toilet. He's a total toilet character.

In this case the bathtub is a euphemism for the toilet. A toilet in all languages is symbolic of death. If a guy's head is in a toilet, do you hear him talking? In other words, that's how much I'm listening to you. *Ich hob zol in bod.*

Actually, you're not wishing for him to be dead. *Ich hob zol in bod* is not quite hoping for a drowning. You just want him to be in a position where he can't holler for help. If he's in a tub of water, at least I won't hear him. Let him stay alive somewhere, but not in my neighborhood.

In Drerd Mein Gelt:
pronounced, EEN DREHRD MINE GELT

Literally it means "My money went to hell." In other words, my money went down the drain. It's the saying of every Jewish husband whose wife has a credit card. *In drerd mein gelt* is what every Jew says every time his wife leaves the house to go shopping. No matter where she goes, he knows it's going to be *in drerd mein gelt.* Any time his wife says, "Good afternoon, honey." She doesn't have to say she's going shopping. He knows. And he knows what that's going to mean to his money. He slaps his forehead and mutters to himself, *"In drerd mein gelt!"*

Every time a wife takes the new car out for a ride, the husband is imagining crashes all over the country.

When she wants to prepare the wedding for her daughter and says, "Don't worry, I won't spend a lot of money," he knows better.

A parent sends his kid to college for an education. But

as it turns out, the parent is the one getting the education. The kid doesn't learn anything, but the parents—oy!—they're learning every day that it's *in drerd mein gelt*.

What kids study in college is how to get more money from their parents. They're learning how to come up with excuses for a bigger allowance. You learn that not only are you spending money on your son, you're supporting three of his girlfriends, too.

There's no kid that goes to college today because he wants to learn something. He's going there because he wants to get away from his parents. No matter how great the colleges are in the neighborhood, he never finds a college nearby. No college that is anywhere close to where his parents live is good enough for him. No matter where you are—you could be in the middle of forty-seven colleges—and all of a sudden you find out that the only college that's good for him is in Arizona. That's when you know it's *in drerd mein gelt*.

Kishkes:
pronounced, KISH-kess

ishkes, literally translated, are the guts or the intestines, but figuratively speaking it's when you feel something in the deepest part of your body. It's the most profound emotion. When, for example, a father hears that his thirty-five-year-old daughter is finally getting married, he feels a happiness from the *kishkes*.

It's being surprised with a $3,000 return from the IRS.

It's opening the paper and getting a great review.

It's a woman flying across a store and grabbing the last dress on sale.

Those are times when you feel a thrill from the *kishkes*.

Klutz:
pronounced to rhyme with "butts"

A *klutz* is so clumsy, so awkward, such a bungler that he can do nothing right. When he tries to wind his watch, he breaks it. If he visits friends in their backyard, he'll fall into their pool. His foot is always sticking out so somebody can trip over it.

When he takes a girl on a date, and puts on his raincoat, he hits her with the buckle and blinds her for a month.

If he's helping somebody move a piano, he pushes it right through a wall.

He'll use somebody's phone and it drops on their antique marble table that cost $10,000 and breaks it. When he sits down to patch up the table, he breaks the arm of their original Louis XIV chair. When he finally leaves, he closes the door and the knob comes off in his hand.

You can't take a *klutz* anywhere.

Kochleffl:
pronounced, KOOCH-leffel

A *kochleffl* is a busybody, a man- or woman-about-town. He's a combination of Walter Winchell and a plain *yenta*. A *kochleffl* is a gossip columnist without a column. It's the kind of person who saves you the trouble of reading the paper. It's somebody who knows what's going on all over town.

Kochleffl is the German word for a long wooden spoon, and it's used to stir things, like at the bottom of a pot of vegetable soup. For a person, it's a stirrer-upper, too, but also it's one who's there when the stirring is going on. A kind of eyewitness to it, someone in the thick of things.

But a *kochleffl* is not a person without dignity or self-respect. "She's a real *kochleffl*" is more a term of respect than derision. If you want information on a subject you never heard of, a *kochleffl* knows about it. Not only knows about it, but what time it happened, where it's going on, and who it's going on with.

No matter what you're talking about, a *kochleffl* has either heard about it or was there or will take charge of it or was once in charge of it. A *yenta* spends most of her time trying to louse other people up. The worse things are with other people, the happier the *yenta* is. But a *kochleffl* doesn't necessarily mean any harm, she just wants to be involved in every activity, in every direction, and in every room.

A *kochleffl* doesn't wait to find out what's going on, doesn't wait for the news, because the *kochleffl* is part of the news.

A *kochleffl* is never a member of a committee—she's always the chairlady. She's the chairlady of committees that

69

nobody even formed yet. For reasons no one heard of. But before anybody knows what happened, she's taken over as boss. She always surprises you with information, because you can't figure out where she got it from. She finds out because she talks to everybody, and she talks to people whether she knows them or not. She has the ability to become anyone's confidante, even total strangers.

Someone asks you, "Where are you going tonight?" And a *kochleffl* tells you exactly where, and what time. And all of a sudden she's in charge of the trip. You keep wondering how she even got involved. You never asked her, you don't even know who she is. She just took over.

The only way to control a *kochleffl* is by getting out of town as fast as possible or by taking up a collection to get *her* out of town. Another way is to get yourself a dark room where she can't locate you. Put the lights out and then try to sneak out of the building. The chances are she'll find you. *Kochleffls* always find out, one way or another.

Kvetch:
rhymes with "stretch"

There's a whole class of Jewish people who are *kvetches*. They can't be comfortable no matter what. They're always *kvetching*, or complaining. It's a way of attracting sympathy and attention. So they always have to say or pretend they're sick or dying. They can't depend on intelligence to interest you, or their personality or warmth or concern. So, they *kvetch*.

70

No matter when you say hello to them, something either hurts them or is about to hurt them. If nothing hurts, they don't understand why nothing hurts, it could have hurt, it should have hurt, it used to hurt. No matter where they are, every part of their body is always in trouble. If their foot is okay, then their head hurts. If their head is okay, then their finger has a lot of pain. All of a sudden, their second toe feels a little crooked to them. There's always something that feels strange. They always hear a buzzing in the ear: "There's something buzzing. I don't know what."

There are certain parts of their body that are always safe to pick on. They can always imagine something hurting there. You always have a tooth that's somehow bothering you. Or the stomach is rumbling. Or you woke up and you couldn't move your neck this morning. A lot of pain starts with *kvetches* who are about forty-five and not married yet. All of a sudden, things start to hurt all over. They can't comprehend that they're miserable because they have no sex life. So they develop aches and pains all over.

If a man finds someone who is attracted to him for ten minutes and they make love, then nothing would bother him. But it's different when you reach middle age and haven't had sex in twenty years.

As *kvetches* get older, they imagine more aches and pains. Since Medicaid, they're all in hospitals or doctors' offices. If they have no insurance, they'll just sit in the house and complain. But as soon as they find out they're insured, they're in doctors' offices day and night. Every five minutes there's a different complaint. "There's something on the bottom of my thigh. Every time I move my foot, it lands on the floor. I can't figure it out. Every time I pick up the spoon, Doctor, my mouth opens. I don't know what it is."

Lantsman:
pronounced, LONTS-man

A *lantsman* is literally a person from the same country as you. It's a way of calling someone a brother when you're not related. He comes from the same neighborhood, from the same town. They have the same background. Jews always had a strong affinity toward the people from their own hometown because that's where they suffered together and developed a common identity. They married from within the town and, for most, never left. Jews in the old world were never a very mobile society. They couldn't afford to move any other place, and they couldn't find a safe haven any other place, so they stayed in that place, generation after generation.

Jews had a fierce pride in where they came from. So if you left for a foreign country and, once there, met someone from the same hometown, immediately there were three Jews hugging and kissing for an hour. *"Lantsman! Lantsman!"* They couldn't get over that you came from *their* neighborhood.

If someone else robs you, he's a crook. But if a *lantsman* robs you, then you have to forgive him like a brother or a sister. When a man is trying to get something for nothing he could always use the word *lantsman* to impose on you. When a guy feels he doesn't deserve something but expects you to give it to him anyway, he uses *lantsman* and gets what he wants.

It has become a weapon used all over New York City. When I was a kid, I remember that if you were buying a suit and were in a bargaining position you looked for a store owned by someone from your hometown in Europe. When the bar-

72

gaining got down to $12 and you couldn't get it any lower, you say, "Where are you from?"

The store owner says, "Varsha."

"Varsha!? I'm from Varsha!"

"You're from Varsha?! *Lantsman!* Eight dollars."

It could be Minsk. It could be Geburnya. It was like, "What? How can you make a profit from your brother?"

From a social standpoint, *lantsman* is also very important. Your son, for instance, is going out with a girl and everyone in the family says, "Ech, she's ugly, she's stupid." Then your son says that she's from the same town as the family was from. All of a sudden, everything changes: "Oy, what a lovely girl!" The fat, stupid person immediately becomes slim and beautiful and brilliant. Now the families can have something in common after the marriage.

Even among Jews, with all the love and the concern they have for each other as a people, the fact is that Jews are always divided among nationalities and groups. A Litvak never really wants his daughter to marry a Galitzianer, or a Russian Jew a Rumanian Jew. It isn't as bad as marrying a gentile, but it isn't the same Jew.

As with other people, there are always status symbols among Jews, even, of course, within their own communities and within the same *lantsmen* themselves. If a father is a rabbi, for example, and his daughter is interested in a tailor's son, he'd say "Yeech, a *schneider's zeen?* He works with his hands?" There is also always a question of *yichus*, of status, of what kind of family the child came from. That is more important than the child itself. They act like the families are marrying each other, not the children.

In America, today's status symbol is usually money. In Europe, money was an important status symbol, but most revered was the family tree. Jews in Europe were so involved in preserving the dignity of the family and the status of the family that the question always was, "What kind of a family does he come from?" If the boy came from a shoemaker's family or a tailor's family, rather than the family of a rabbi or a great entrepreneur or the man who owned the dry goods store, the family was embarrassed. It was as if somebody had leprosy in that family and if your son or daughter married the other person, everybody in your family would wind up in a leper colony. It got everybody nauseated right away.

Despite all this, *lantsman* has great significance when you leave your hometown. As a Jew, you feel responsible for a *lantsman*. There is magic in the word. People on all levels of the economic ladder understand the concept.

When a beggar in America comes to your house and asks for a bowl of soup, he always tries to find out which town you came from first. If you say it is the same town that he could also claim, you not only give him soup, you give him a shirt, a tie, a pair of pants, and you give him a month's rent, too.

Litvaks and Galitzianers:
pronounced very much as they look

These are names for Jews from Lithuania and Galicia—Galicia having been a province in Poland and then in Austria, when Austria took control of it. Lithuania and Galicia were neighbors and both were heavily populated with Jews, and the Jews had fierce loyalties to their regions. It is like the rivalries between the Russian Jews and the Hungarian Jews, or the White Russian Jews against the

Jews from the Ukraine. There were divisions and there were jealousies and pride in their own groups. Each group convinced itself it was better than the other group. *"Oy,"* one of them might say, "look at that Rumanian *chozzer."* (That greedy Rumanian pig.)

It's no different from this country. Southerners always look at Northerners with disdain and jealousy. Northerners think that Southerners are ignorant. Most people outside of New York think of New Yorkers as hustlers, as con men, as liars, cheats, and thieves. Meanwhile, New Yorkers think of Midwesterners as drab, colorless people with no personality. Everyone thinks that everyone in New York is in a hurry. New Yorkers think everyone else moves too slowly.

If a New Yorker switches his residence to another part of the country, all of a sudden he makes an attribute of what he always thought was a liability. A New Yorker thinks of a Californian, for example, as someone wasting his time, sitting by his pool, hanging around like a dummy, seeing nothing, hearing nothing, and going nowhere. He's got smog and dirt and traffic.

But if a New Yorker moves to California, within six months everything changes. Now he says, "I hate New York. I don't know what I was ever doing in New York. The filth of New York, the *dreck.* There's nothing but crime and dirt and garbage. Look what we have here. We have green, we have shrubbery, we have sunshine, we have a swimming pool!"

The fact is that this ex–New Yorker will never use his pool and will never even go into his pool. He has nothing to do with it. When he finds a charcoal broiler he invites everybody over and they eat from the charcoal broiler, look at the pool, and convince each other that they went somewhere.

This becomes the way of life for every Jewish Californian. The husband and wife sit a foot-and-a-half apart and they're bored to death. So are all the friends who come over. Everyone says how proud and happy they are to be there because they can get together. It's either your pool or their pool. The whole world consists of two pools and a tennis court. And they never play tennis, either.

I could understand pools for gentiles, because gentiles actually swim in their pools and they play tennis, too. But Jews just use these things to show another Jew that they can afford it. Once they've showed you they can afford it, they don't have to use it. Gentiles buy things to use. Jews buy things to afford. "You know what else I could afford? Look what else I got."

As soon as a Jew buys something, the other guy buys something else that he thinks you can't afford. They're involved in a contest that they're not even aware of.

If you ask a Jew, "What do you have?" he'll answer, "A thirty-two-room house." It's the most stunning house, it's so gorgeous, he can't get over it. Until he finds out you've got thirty-six rooms. Now all of a sudden he needs thirty-eight.

Some people were thrilled to buy a house for $85,000 when they were thirty years old. But that's twenty years ago. The family didn't get any bigger, but he got an $8 raise and he thought he could stretch himself into a $112,000 house because now, he says, he'll have the extra room he's always wanted.

It's a common occurrence. Then they want a second bedroom to be more furnished compared to the first bedroom, compared to the third bedroom, and compared to the living room. And then he wants to find out if he can afford a house in a certain area in Great Neck where there is a whole row of $300,000 houses.

When he moves into his new house, he gets a completely different list. He has a sauna in one room, and in another

76

room he has those weight-lifting *tchotchkes*, and a bicycle that doesn't move.

He never uses the sauna, never touches the exercise equipment, but he's able to show you two extra rooms that have no purpose at all. And in one of these rooms he has a long table with Chinese figurines on it with thirty-seven chairs. And this Chinese room becomes the most untouched room there ever was. Every Jewish house has that Chinese room on the side with a picture on the wall of a Chinese man standing with a sword. Nobody goes in this Chinese museum room. It is the room for the special occasion, so special that no one will ever live to see it.

No matter how many rooms Jews have, they always want one more. They're always one room short.

People always subconsciously need a way to feel superior to somebody else. So they invent ways to satisfy themselves. Other people don't have the qualities you have because they're from the wrong neighborhood, they're the wrong color, they're the wrong something. That's why, even when you break it down to Jews, who are supposedly close to each other, everyone finds ways and excuses to compete with each other.

Getting back to the *Litvaks* and the *Galitzianers*, you see that everybody is involved in one kind of competition or another, one status symbol or another. If you're Jewish without a status symbol, you don't feel Jewish. Without being involved in a contest, you can't be a Jew. Jews are born to compete. They're born to be involved in a race with every other Jew and every other gentile, with everybody. That's why, when you show a gentile a chair, he sits in it. When you show a Jew a chair, he gets into a fight about it. "You call this a chair? I've got a chair at home you would never believe."

When a gentile goes to the theater, he asks at the window, "Do you have any seats in the front for this price?" A

Jew says, "Let me see the chart." They all want to see the theater seating chart. Then they all study it with a critical eye. And no matter which seat you show them on the chart, that's not the one they want.

That's because Jews are involved in a race. They always know that somebody somewhere has a closer seat or a lower price or a bigger living room or a higher chair or a faster exercise bike. And it gets him nauseated. And that goes double if the other person is a *Galitzianer* and you're a *Litvak*.

Loch in Kop:
||||||||||||||||||||||||||||||||||||||||||||||||
pronounced, LOKH en kohp

*I*t's a hole in the head, as in, "I need this like a hole in the head."

When the stock market takes a plunge, every Jew is holding his head and running around saying the same thing, "I need this like a *loch in kop*."

It's a typical thing that Jews say about partners in business. Each partner thinks that he's the only one who is necessary. No matter how much the other partner has been making for the business, the first guy is convinced that his partner is out to break him. He can do better without him, and if he doesn't get rid of him soon they're going to get wiped out. He says, "I need him like a *loch in kop*." And then the partner gets a cold on top of everything. "I need *this* like a *loch in kop*." And then his wife hangs up on him, and that's one more thing he needs like a *loch in kop*.

There are numerous examples of needing something like

78

a *loch in kop:* You make love to the most stunning girl you've ever seen; you think it's worth more than anything in the world, and when you come home afterward, you see pimples.

You send your daughter to college and with hopes that she'll marry a doctor. You give her all the money she wants. Then one night, she calls with the news that she's eloped with a bongo player.

A guy buys an expensive suit with two pairs of pants, and burns a hole in the jacket. "This," he says, "I need like a *loch in kop.*"

Machen a Tzimmis:
pronounced, MAKH-en ah TSIM-is

When you make a big fuss about something, a big issue, a big tumult, that's called a *machen a tzimmis.* A *tzimmis* is a compote, a side dish of cooked fruits and vegetables. It's a kind of commotion or a mixture of fruits. And *machen* is "making."

Machen a tzimmis is the taking of extraneous issues— irrelevant, unnecessary issues—and blowing them up into a significance that is undeserving. It's preparing a whole stew when all you wanted was a carrot. In other words, it's making a mountain out of a molehill.

It's also a way of getting out of a jam. Every time a guy is caught with crooked goods and he wants to whitewash it, he'll always say, "You're making a whole *tzimmis* out of nothing."

It is all a matter of perspective, two people with different views. Every time one Jew gets excited, there's always another Jew saying, "Don't make such a *tzimmis.*"

Unless it's happening to you, it is always nothing. A Jew who tries to park a car into a space usually has a *yenta* sitting next to him and directing: "Turn it to the left! Turn it to the right! *Oy,* you missed it! What's taking you so long? *Oy, a klug,* not so fast, not so short, not so loud, you could have had it before!" Every husband is yelling, "Don't make such a *tzimmis,* you big *yenta.*" *Tzimmis* often goes together with a phrase like "big *yenta.*"

In another instance, the father tells his son he needs a haircut. His hair is not only a little long to the father, it's an ugly mess. "Howie, you got to get a haircut. Do you know how you look? How terrible, how disgusting, how nauseating?" He builds it up so that because of the hair the son is a menace to society. And the son can't figure out what this whole *tzimmis* is all about.

Another example: You're waiting to make love to your girlfriend and she's putting on perfume and primping her hair and going in and out of the bedroom and you're just dying for her. She's still preparing and organizing and changing and rearranging. You can't take it anymore. You holler, "What are you making a whole *tzimmis* for?"

Macher:
pronounced, MAH-kher

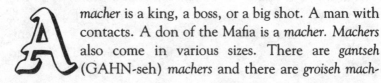 *macher* is a king, a boss, or a big shot. A man with contacts. A don of the Mafia is a *macher. Machers* also come in various sizes. There are *gantseh* (GAHN-seh) *machers* and there are *groiseh mach-*

ers. That's big, bigger, and biggest. But the phrase *gantseh macher* is usually used to make fun of a guy who *thinks* he's a boss. You say, "Hey, look at this *gantseh macher*." It means, "Give a look at this guy, he thinks he's such a big deal." But a *groiseh macher* is truly a big deal, he's a real *macher*.

A *gantseh macher* is someone who has never made it, but can't believe he hasn't and keeps thinking of himself as a *macher*. A Jewish waiter, for example, usually becomes a *gantseh macher* because he usually thinks he's running the restaurant.

A gentile taxi driver says, "How do you like that, I got a job." But a Jewish taxi driver has a different view. He can't believe he's driving a taxi so he convinces himself that this is only one of a thousand taxis he could have bought. He believes that when you get in the taxi, you're not the passenger, he is, and that you're really the driver. He just happens to be sitting in the front seat by a freak accident, or that the back is too crowded, or that there are too many fumes in the rear. He tells you, "The air is fresher in the front. I always sit up here."

A gentile taxi driver doesn't talk, he listens. But every time I get into a taxi with a Jew who is driving, I'm listening for an hour.

A Jewish taxi driver doesn't even ask where I'm going. He takes me where *he* wants to go, and he tells me off all the way there. He tells me why I'm wrong and why I never amounted to anything. Why he's driving a taxi, he'll never know. He's taking me as a personal favor. He's got businesses everywhere that are doing wonderful, thank God.

There are more *gantseh machers* driving taxi cabs than in any other profession in the world.

Maven:
||||||||||||||||||||||||||||||
pronounced, MAY-vin

A *maven* is an expert, and it's something that every Jew thinks he is on every subject that exists. A *maven* is someone who knows everything. And if he doesn't he would never admit it. If he's not an expert on every subject, then he either had to convert, or he passed away fifty years ago.

Any Jew who is not a *maven* automatically loses his right to be a Jew. He automatically loses his membership in his temple, too. A Jew becomes a *maven* not because he learned the subject, but because someone asked his opinion.

A *maven* is one of the major differences between Jews and gentiles. Gentiles at least let you finish a question before they give you the answer. A Jew gives you an answer whether he knows the question or not. A gentile has to find out about it, a Jew is an expert even if he never heard of it.

A Jew may know absolutely nothing about opera, but when you bring him there, he's a *maven*. When you ask how this is possible when he didn't know an opera from a tse-tse fly, he gives you one answer that puts you in your place: "Never mind."

Same kind of thing will happen if someone buys an elephant. If he asks, "What do you think of this elephant?" a Jew is the only one who will have an answer. It makes no difference that the only elephant he ever saw was in a Tarzan movie, because now he tells you whether you got a bargain or not, what it's worth, and where you could have bought the elephant for a cheaper price.

A Jew is the natural *maven*. From the day he's born, he becomes a *maven* in every field. Even before a Jew can talk, he already has an opinion and he can't tell it to you yet. But just wait!

Did you ever show a Jew something and he couldn't tell you whether it was good or bad? Or if it's going to work or not? That's why, whenever a Jew buys something, he always takes another Jew with him. He'll never take a gentile because a gentile might say he's not sure about it. Every time a Jew wants to buy a house, he takes another Jew along. A gentile takes an appraiser, a Jew takes a *maven*. An appraiser shows up with rulers and yardsticks and wrenches and magnifying glasses. A maven comes in and knocks on a wall, opens a window, and measures off the distance in a room by putting one foot in front of the other. An appraiser takes six weeks to figure out an answer. A *maven* tells you in seventeen seconds.

Economists are always *mavens*. An economist tells you what's going to happen and then explains to you why it didn't. Politicians aren't *mavens* because they're always trying to find out what you think first, and then they agree with you.

The economist tells you first that the stock market is going to go up. Then when it goes down, he says that that's not what he meant. And if he meant it, you didn't understand it because it's not his fault that he said it.

It's always because something happened that wasn't supposed to happen. The incident is at fault. The country is at fault, the currency's at fault, everything is at fault except what the *maven* was predicting. If the world had stayed the same, things would never have happened as they did. He can't manage the world. He can only manage the prediction. So if you mix him up, it's not his fault.

The *maven* is never confused by the facts. He is never confused by information. He's never confused by anything, which is why he's always right, even when he's wrong.

83

Mazel Tov:
pronounced, MAH-zel toff

Whenever somebody accomplishes something that calls for a celebration, you have a *mazel tov*. You always shout *"mazel tov!"* whenever anything good happens. It's good luck, loads of luck, congratulations, that's terrific, what a fabulous thing! *"Mazel tov!"* You invest $50 in a stock that you never heard of and a year later you find out it actually made money. Not only did it make money, but you were also able to send your son to medical school. That's a *mazel tov*.

If the *bar mitzvah* pays for itself from the presents, it's a *mazel tov*.

And if you happened to get off the *Titanic* in time, then that's a double *mazel tov*.

Mecheieh:
pronounced, meh-KHY-eh

It's a pleasure!" That's what *mecheieh* means. It is used in a variety of situations. "Oy, it's a *mecheieh*!" can be heard when somebody is drinking a cup of coffee or after sex or anywhere in-between. You're lying under a truck and you can't get out. Somebody comes by and picks up the truck. "What a *mecheieh*!" When a girl comes along to make love to you on top of that, that's an even greater *mecheieh*.

The word is also often used to express relief from human misery. A man is walking around a subway station looking for a men's room for a week-and-a-half. When he finally finds one, "Oy, a *mecheieh*."

It's used when you find a fresh roll under a basket of stale ones. Or your umbrella finally opens in the rain. Or your mother-in-law stops talking for five seconds.

If a guy is sweating in 90-degree weather, and walks into an air-conditioned room when he wasn't expecting it, immediately every Jew will say the same thing, "Ay, a *mecheieh!*" They talk to the room. A *mecheieh* is something that's such a pleasure you don't have to have a person in front of you to tell it to. When a Jew says, "a *mecheieh*," there's likely to be no one else there. The pleasures are something that he can't wait to bless and he can't wait for anybody to listen to. If you're around a Jew and he exclaims, "Ay, a *mecheieh!*" and you ask, "Who are you talking to?" you can bet he'll say, "Oh, I'm talking to myself. Who knew you were listening? I just wanted to hear myself. I couldn't get over what a good time I'm having."

Mensh, or Mench:
rhymes with "clench"

ensh literally means "a person," a human being, but the broader meaning is a human being with class, with feelings, and with a sense of humanity. In other words, a *mensh* is a gentleman. If you ask someone for a loan and he turns you down, the man's a *schmuck*, who needs him? But if he lends you the money right away, this is a *mensh*. He should live a long life.

Any time someone wants to give the ultimate compliment to a person, he'll say, "Oh, this is a *mensh*." A *mensh* means a person of honor and integrity, an upstanding citizen. If a politician, for example, is behind in an election but still can't bring himself to say a bad word about his opponent, people say, "Ooh, this is a *mensh*." There are no such politicians, of course, but if there was one, people would call him a *mensh*.

A man finds, for example, that a friend opens a competitive store across the street, and now all of a sudden he's not making a quarter. He's practically wiped out, but instead of telling the guy to drop dead, he sends him a letter of congratulations for being such a hit. People will say, "Oh, this man's a *mensh*." Of course, some others say, "This man's an idiot." But the kinds of things an average person might do to express vengeance or hate or contempt or any kind of severity of emotions, the *mensh* doesn't do. The *mensh* is in ultimate control.

This is a man or a woman who never is involved in self-indulgence. They wouldn't even try to get even with you no matter what you did to them. When they see the opportunity is there to bury somebody, to get even with somebody, to wipe out somebody, top somebody, they don't take it. They can't. It's not in their character.

If your mother-in-law comes to your house for the weekend and then decides to stay a month, a normal person would grab her by the throat. But the *mensh* composes himself and says, "I'm happy to hear it." A *mensh* sacrifices his own needs, his own pleasures, his own advantages, his own ambitions for somebody else. Any way that you see a person make any display of gentility in the face of a bad predicament, in the face of an insult, in the face of danger, in the face of collusion or

86

corruption, you see a *mensh*. When he has the opportunity to tell you off and does nothing, this is a *mensh*.

Mensh Tracht und Gott Lacht:
pronounced like it looks

It means "man plans and God laughs."

This is the ultimate answer on whether or not you're going to succeed. It won't come from you, it's going to come from God. God is laughing at your efforts because the future is really in his hands and it's up to him and not you to decide the outcome of things.

You do your best and sometimes God will allow you to come to something, and sometimes he won't. This is a great way to accomplish two things: You can prove you're religious, that you believe in God; and at the same time you can excuse yourself for being a total idiot.

It's a way of exonerating yourself from failure. Every time a guy stinks at something, he says, "*Mensh tracht und Gott lacht.*" You're saying, "God decided against it. It's not that I'm a *shmuck*. The fact that I thought I could open a $30 million restaurant on $300 doesn't make me stupid. It's God's fault. He didn't want me to have such a big restaurant."

Anything can happen to a Jew in the universe. Anything can cave in at a moment's notice. And nobody knows where it came from or who to attribute it to. They need some explanation, some rationalization, something to hang their hat on and maintain their sanity. So they attribute whatever happens to God. He had some kind of plan that you never heard about. But God doesn't call you up or consult you before he does things, and there's no way to get in touch with him to find out what he has in mind next.

You could have done everything right. You could have saved up your whole life and now you're deciding where to buy the safest farm in the world. You're studying seismology, geography, technology, and you find out where an earthquake could never hit in a million years. You build the farm and move in and ten seconds later there's an earthquake. Nothing like this ever happened in that neighborhood before. I'm sweating but meanwhile God does what he pleases, and I wind up in the soup.

So how do you get God on your side? Jews think that you must be a devout person, that you must be a symbol of decency, humanity, love, brotherhood, and honesty. You must avoid everything that conflicts with God's intentions for mankind. If you abide by his regulations, his scriptures and his advice about human behavior, then only good will come of it.

Now take those landlords who give thousands of dollars to charity but then evict a one-hundred-year-old lady. These landlords are in violation of the basic precepts of religion and decency, and God will deal with them as he sees fit. This applies not just to Jews, but to all people.

Every time I saw a pretty girl and wanted to follow her, my father would say, "Forget about it." Because *Gott lacht*. To him, it was a violation of the rules of God to try to fool around with girls unless you're married—a religious man is not allowed to touch a girl that he's not married to. It was forbidden fruit, and since no one has figured out how to make love to a girl without touching her, my father was trying to save me time, effort, and expense. I knew that I would be spending money on waitresses and hatcheck girls and models, and he knew that my money could go for better causes, like to the *shul*, or for poor people on Passover.

In the final analysis, Jews believe that you don't control your fate. God does. And the laughter you hear after you've made all your elaborate plans is the laughter of God.

Meshuggener:
pronounced, meh-SHOOG-en-er

This term covers anybody you consider nuts. When you call someone a *meshuggener* (or female *meshuggeneh*), you're saying he's beyond stupid, but you're saying it in a playful and colloquial way. If, for example, you borrow money from somebody and you promise to pay him back in a month, and the month passes and he actually comes to collect his money, that's a *meshuggener*.

A *meshuggener* sees an article in the newspaper about a state dinner at the White House on Tuesday. He shows up in a tuxedo and gets mad when they won't let him in. "I'm an American citizen," he says, "I pay my taxes. And I'm hungry."

A man wants to have sex with his wife. "Are you a *meshuggener*?" she says. "We just had sex a month ago."

A man sees John Gotti about to park his car in a space, and then decides to beat him to it. That's a real *meshuggener*.

Meshuggeneh Velt:
pronounced, meh-SHOOG-en-eh velt

I t means "crazy world." It's so crazy that God only knows why things happen the way they do. Some occurrences are just beyond explanation. You tried forty-six ways to figure it out and nothing makes sense. So your conclusion is that the world is upside down and turned around. You see a beautiful girl with an ugly guy and you ask, "What does she see in him?" Or an idiot becomes rich. All you can say is, "A *meshuggeneh velt.*"

Mieskeit:
pronounced, MEES-kite

ieskeit means "ugly."
 Every Jewish mother is hoping and waiting for her son to get married, and as soon as she hears that he might be a little serious about a girl, she says, "Oh, I'm delighted to hear it. I'm so happy. I can't wait until you bring her home so I can meet her." When the son brings the girl over and the mother opens the door, every Jewish mother says the same thing, "Oh, I've heard so much about you. I'm pleased to meet you." Ten seconds later she turns to her son and says, "Yech, a *mieskeit.*" The mother says this about the girl even if she looks like Raquel Welch.
 Mieskeit is not quiet enough of an opinion for the mother. She has to add, "This is the girl you picked? A man like you? Every girl in the world is dying for you and you pick her? You

90

have the nerve to bring her here, and in the daylight? Aren't you ashamed?" The son shrugs. The mother says, "I'm only interested in your happiness. It's not my business. But I can't believe it. But I don't mix in. It's your life," and then she walks away, muttering, "Ay, such a *mieskeit.*"

A Jewish mother is always looking for somebody better for her son, even though no one better exists. The mother also feels threatened that she'd be losing a son. Meanwhile, her son Ralph is an emaciated *shlepper* with pimples. Women aren't exactly following him around. The mother should thank God that somebody even looks at him. But to her, he's stunning and the girl, no matter who she is, is a *mieskeit.*

You also hear the word *mieskeit* around babies a lot. According to a grandmother, all other babies are *mieskeits* except her granddaughter. By coincidence the only *shaineh,* or pretty baby, in the world just happens to be hers. Every new baby is the ugliest thing—they are so disgusting, they're impossible to look at, the face is ugly, the eyes are crooked, the noses are red, the head is flat. But my baby granddaughter? "My God, nobody could stop looking at her! Everybody wanted to pick her up and kiss her. They wouldn't leave her alone. Nobody could tear themselves away from that baby!"

The fact is, everybody who looked at her reacted as they do with other babies—they ran like a thief. There was only one person who couldn't tear herself away from that baby, and that was the grandmother.

Mishegoss:
pronounced, mish-eh-GOSS

This is insanity, madness, irrational behavior, or a total figment of your imagination. "It's just your *mishegoss*," is a common expression when someone is caught in the act of a misdeed.

A man makes a play for the maid, and the wife notices something funny going on. He tells her, "Oh, get that *mishegoss* out of your head." The wife says, "But I saw you mopping the floor for her. Why are you doing her work for her?"

He says, "What work? I wasn't mopping anything. I found the mop on the floor and I moved it. The mop was in my way. So I moved it over. Can I help it if I had to move it three hundred times? I couldn't get it where I wanted it."

Or a wife wants a nose job and the husband doesn't want to spend the money, but he doesn't want to come off looking cheap, either. He says, "You look beautiful. It's a perfect nose. A nose like that you see only in the movies."

She says, "But look, isn't it a little funny looking and crooked?"

He tells her, "Such a nose I can't believe. It's absolutely stunning. You gotta talk yourself out of this *mishegoss*." Meanwhile, the nose starts in New York and ends in Turkey, but he's desperate to save $5,000.

Mishpocheh:
pronounced, mis-POH-kheh

ishpocheh means family. The family is always the holiest unit for Jews because it was one of their few sources of encouragement in the universe.

When you ask a gentile, "How's the family?" you get a different response than when you ask a Jew the same question. Gentiles don't really think of the question as really important. It's just a term of greeting, a conversation filler. It's like, "How are you?" The person is not actually wondering how you are. Because if you told him, he'd kill himself. But for Jews two questions always follow each other: "How are you? How's the family?" and once you start answering, they stop listening.

When a friend asks, "So how's the family?" and the Jew answers, "Don't ask!" he will then tell you anyway—for three hours. The most dangerous thing for a Jew is one word about the *mishpocheh* because he's always dying to tell you.

You think you're only asking a concerned question, but he thinks he's found a captive audience. If you happen not to use the word *mishpocheh* right away, he'll be listening for it for the next hour and a half, because there's no way you can get away from the other Jew, especially if he has two children. And if one's a doctor, you're there all day.

If the other one is not a doctor, but only a bookkeeper, he'll elevate him to an accountant. He'll always find some way to make him grow into some great professional accomplishment. If his son is a pushcart peddler, he's in marketing. If he's a post office worker, he owns the post office. If he's a prisoner, he works for the government.

So when a guy talks about his *mishpocheh*, it's often a

93

gantseh mishpocheh, or a *groiseh mishpocheh*—a big family and an even bigger family.

Poor people usually have small *mishpocheh.* But if a man starts making money, then everybody will find some way to become related to him. If you're earning $300 a week, your brother-in-law is the only relative you have. If you're making $1,000 a week, it's the brother-in-law and his relatives. If you make $10,000 a week, it's the brother-in-law and his relatives and the town commissioner of the city he lives in.

That's how a *mishpocheh* grows. A guy who's finally earning a decent living doesn't understand how the *mishpocheh* got to be a *gantseh mishpocheh* and then a *groiseh mishpocheh.* Just when he thinks he's got to the bottom of it, more *mishpocheh* start showing up.

Mitzvah:
pronounced, MITS-veh

itzvah is a Hebrew word for good deed. Every time you do a good deed it's called a *mitzvah.* If you help any person for whatever reason, it's a *mitzvah.* If a girl wants to make love and has nobody to make love to, and you make love to her, you're doing a *mitzvah.* That's why I try to make love to everybody I see.

If someone who has no collateral asks you for a loan because no bank will give him one, and you help him out, then that, too, is a *mitzvah.* One thing about someone who

94

does a lot of *mitzvahs*, he usually goes broke because nobody pays him back.

Among religious Jews, the most worthy are those who perform *mitzvahs*. They believe that it is their moral obligation before God. It's the hallmark of every orthodox Jew that he should do as many *mitzvahs* as possible. He feels it is his moral obligation before God, and the truly orthodox Jew never asks what's in it for him. That's why to this day the Jews are the biggest charity givers of any denomination in the world. The accent in Jewish culture and Jewish religion was always on doing *mitzvahs* to help the underdog.

That's why you'll notice that even though Jews in general make a more comfortable living than most other groups, Jews overall remain Democrats. Even the Jews who are the richest in America often can't force themselves to become Republicans. In other denominations, if someone makes more than, say, $100,000 a year, you'll find that he's usually a Republican. Why are most Jews still Democrats? Because the Jewish conscience is still with the underdog.

The Jew remains liberal in his heart, and a defender of those who might be considered less fortunate. When someone seeks to help anyone in circumstances less fortunate than his own, it is called a *mitzvah*.

But it can work the opposite way, too. It's easier to take advantage of him. That's why when you hit the Jew over the head with a pipe, he wonders what your problem is and how to help you. A gentile wonders how he could hit you back over the head with a pipe. A Jew wants to take you to a psychiatrist because you need help. Every time a Jew is bleeding like a dog, you see a criminal going to a psychiatrist. And the Jew is paying for it.

Naches:
pronounced, NOKH-ess

aches is joy, delight, happiness, but it goes even deeper, it's pleasure. One of the greatest things a Jew can experience is a pride so deep that he feels it all the way into his *kishkes*, into the deepest recesses of his intestines. Jews are always saying to other Jews, "You should only know *naches* from your children. Your children should only be successful. They should be healthy and happy."

Children primarily are the ones from whom *naches* is generated and felt. If a daughter should marry a doctor, that's great. But if he's a specialist, that's even better. And if he should own a medical center on top of that, then the *naches* is nearly beyond words.

Naye Geshichta:
pronounced, Nigh-yuh Geh-SIKH-teh

new story, another tale or yet another piece of fiction.

When someone is trying to put something over on you, you respond, "A *naye geshichta*." As if to say, "Oh, that's a good one." Someone shows up late and gives the excuse that there was too much traffic. That's the first *geshichta*. When you confront him and say the traffic has been there for thirty years, they didn't invent traffic this afternoon, he says, "Ooh, I forgot to tell you, I was also on

96

my way out of the house when I was hit by a bike." Another story. Or "The elevator collapsed." Or "My foot, you see how I'm walking?" Then you say, "It's a *naye geshichta.*"

When the first excuse doesn't work, the guy comes up with another one. "What, you expect me to believe that story?" If it's the first story, it's just a *geshichta.* But the second story, and all the others are a *naye geshichta.*

The husband comes home late and his wife meets him at the door. "Where've you been?" she asks.

"I was on Third Street," he says.

"But I was on Third Street and you weren't there."

"Excuse me, it was Fourth Street."

And that's when you hear, "A *naye geshichte.*"

Neshoma:
pronounced, neh-SHU-mah

Neshoma means "soul," and is usually used with *guta neshoma,* or good soul. It's the inner spirit of man, the essential ingredients of a person. It's an expression that says, "Deep in his heart he's a wonderful human being."

Just as *mensh* refers to his behavior, a *guta neshoma* refers to basic character. It's deeper and richer and more meaningful even than *mensh.* A *guta neshoma* means that a person can't feel hate no matter what.

It's used, for example, to refer to your grandmother. Somehow, when a girl is young, people are suspicious of her. When she's a mother, she's a tyrant. But when she becomes

97

a grandmother, she's always a *guta neshoma*. She's so sweet, it would be impossible for her to do any harm. It so happens in reality that she doesn't have the strength to do any harm.

That's why people ascribe to grandmothers only the kindliest of qualities. A grandmother could be a vicious human being, and could be ready to kill other Jews in the streets, but if she's eighty-seven years old, they say, "Oh, she's a *guta neshoma.*"

Nisht Geferlacht:
‖‖‖‖‖‖‖‖‖‖‖‖‖‖‖‖‖‖‖‖‖‖‖‖‖‖‖‖‖‖‖‖‖‖‖‖‖‖
pronounced, Nisht ge-FER-lacht

Nisht geferlacht means "no big deal." When your children do something wrong, it's *nisht geferlacht*. When you lose thirty-five cents, it's a disaster. You're looking for it under every table. You're asking everybody, "Did you see that thirty-five cents? It was a quarter and two nickles." This is a disaster.

If you get a parking ticket for $2.50, you run down the street after the meter maid. But if somebody else loses $1 million, you tell him, "*Nisht geferlacht*. Is money everything? It's your health that counts." Then if the other guy loses his health, too, that's *nisht geferlacht* because you tell him, "Life is not the most important thing in the world, it's only death that matters." If he dies, it's nobody's fault, it's *nisht geferlacht*, because he had a good life. No matter what happens to him, it's always *nisht geferlacht*. But if you yourself happen to get a toothache, it's the worse calamity in the world.

If you go on your honeymoon and your wife forgot to show up, you call a friend to lament your situation: "Did you hear? I'm on a honeymoon all by myself." You know what the friend would probably say? "*Nisht geferlacht.* Just because you call it a honeymoon, you should be troubled? Meanwhile you're having a nice vacation. You have more room. You have a bed all to yourself. Thank God that nobody is bothering you."

Nisht Geshtoigen, Nisht Gefloigen: pronounced, nisht gesh-TOY-gen, nisht geh-FLOY-gen

This literally means "something doesn't stand, it didn't fly." If it doesn't stand or fly, it doesn't do anything. So obviously it doesn't exist. When Jews use it, it means something that has been said that makes no sense, or has no root in reality.

If you owe somebody $10 and he asks you for it, you want to deny you owe it. "What? You never loaned it!" Or "I paid it back!" If it's $10, you say he's telling a lie. If it's $100, it's a big lie. But if you owe $1,000 you say, *Nisht geshtoigen, nisht gefloigen.* This is the only way to wipe it out completely. It is the ultimate way of saying something never happened. The greatest retort to the biggest lie is, *Nisht geshtoigen, nisht gefloigen.* Not only did it never happen, but you're making a real *schmuck* out of the guy for even *thinking* it!

If you're seen at a *shiksa*'s house on Yom Kippur, and they bring it up in *shul,* you can't say, "I might have been there," or "I could have been," or "You got the wrong guy." You have to exclaim, "Nisht geshtoigen, nisht gefloigen!"

This is to convince everybody that not only is it not true, but the guy who is accusing you is a nut as well. He's seeing things that never happened, that could never possibly happen. He's out of his mind completely. You should not only question the truth of what he's saying, you should question his sanity, too.

Just because you saw it, that's no excuse for believing it. Just because it's true, this is no time to mention it. Even if you catch your wife in bed with another man, she tries to convince you that you're on the wrong track. She says, "It's not what you think. He's only teaching me to dance."

It never happened and it never will. It never sat there and it never flew. It never existed. Not only was it never here, it never was even a stationary item. It never was any part of the universe.

I wanted to be a paratrooper, but there were no planes at the time.

I could have beaten Babe Ruth, but I couldn't find a bat.

When someone says, "I wanted to buy the Empire State Building," you ask, "So what happened?" They answer: "I missed the bus. I took the number 42 bus instead of the number 32 bus in front of Nathan's Restaurant. I got there five minutes after the sale. They would have given me a break, but they wanted a $300 million deal and I was $9 short. They wanted it in cash."

A man tells you his daughter is more beautiful than Elizabeth Taylor ever was. But *nisht geshtoigen, nisht gefloigen* is when he really has developed the lie and starts telling you that not only does she look ten times prettier than Elizabeth Taylor, but everybody from Hollywood was dying for her to

100

be in a picture. He tells you that all the major motion picture companies were chasing her and she had to run away from them because she's such a model of a girl she didn't want to get involved in such a dirty business. He tells you, "Such a business is not for a respectable girl."

That's why she married the butcher across the street. Not only that, she didn't want to leave the family. She would never leave the family for any price, even though she could have become the biggest star in the world today.

Everybody has a fantasy that they convince themselves is the truth, and anybody listening to them knows it's *nisht geshtoigen, nisht gefloigen.* A woman says, "Do you know what my husband could have been today if he wasn't a tailor? He could have been the biggest politician of all time. They wanted him to be a prime minister. He said, 'What prime minister? Prime minister? They work the whole day. Do you think I wanted the headaches?' So what did he become? He became a tailor. He says a tailor has regular hours. He goes home on time. Who wants to be a prime minister?"

Someone asks, "How come your son is a teacher?" A teacher is considered an intellectual job, but a lot of people are embarrassed that their son is a teacher. They feel he should at least be a principal. A doctor is a symbol of success to them. A lawyer, an accountant, they can still be tolerated, but when it comes down to a teacher, a lot of Jewish mothers get embarrassed. To them it's almost as bad as a mechanic. So assuming he becomes a teacher, they all have their excuses for him: "You think he has to be a teacher? Do you know how many countries wanted him as a terrorist? He could have been the biggest terrorist in the world. In the world! When the French foreign legion was picking its top terrorists, they wanted my son in a second! Nobody tops him.

"He can throw, he can run, he can climb trees. Not only

that, you should see him on a waterfall. Best in his field. He can dive like you never saw before. Put him on any mountain and he can jump off in a second. He could have been one of the biggest terrorists in the world today, but he was busy. I told him, 'You have to go to college. You need something to fall back on.' But if he hadn't gone to college, he would have set records for terrorism that nobody would believe."

And she doesn't stop here. She says "But there's not always a reason for terrorists. They're not always doing so hot. Right now, terrorists are big. But who knows what's going to happen to terrorists five years from now? There may be no order for terrorists. This way, my son's got a pension. Do you know that terrorists get no pension? They get no unemployment. You might get off holidays. God forbid they tell you you have to invade Turkey. They don't care if it's Yom Kippur. One thing about being a teacher, he doesn't work on Yom Kippur, no matter what.

"Terrorists have to go on invasions. You can't say you have to start the invasion a week from Monday. An invasion is an invasion. They never hold off an invasion for anybody. This way, if he's got a dental appointment, he goes. There's not a terrorist in the world that can do that. So thank God my son turned down the terrorist movement when they called him at the office, and stayed teaching school."

After listening to this, there's only one thing that you can say to yourself when you walk away: *"Nisht geshtoigen, nisht gefloigen."*

102

Nu:
|||||||||||||
pronounced, new

I t more or less meant the same as "Well?" but if you say, "Well?" in English, it doesn't sound like it means anything. But Jews made *nu* a part of their whole personality. *Nu* became a dynamic word. It's a sound, a rhythm, a whole mood and emotion and moment. It creates an atmosphere. Someone could be asking for something, begging for something, wondering about something, questioning something, challenging something, or even accusing somebody. The interpretation is all in the way it is pronounced. *"Nu?"*

If someone is late for an appointment, you say when they show up, *"Nu?"* If someone invited you to lunch and the check comes and he doesn't make a move to pick it up, you look at him and say, *"Nu?"*

If someone is telling a joke and it's going on and on with no end in sight and you're becoming impatient and sick from it, the listener's last resort is, *"Nu?"* as if to say, "Please God, help him get to the punch line."

Nuchshlepper:
||||||||||||||||||||||||||||||||||||||||||||||||||
pronounced, NOOKH-shlepper.
"Shlepper" rhymes with "pepper"

 A *nuchshlepper* is a straggler or dragger-after. It is someone you meet as soon as you've been appointed to a new job. He sees your name in the paper and notices that you've doubled your salary.

103

That's when the *nuchshlepper* shows up at your house.

He's a relative or an acquaintance you never knew you had who comes from a city you never knew existed for reasons you can't explain, and all of a sudden, there he is: "Hello, hello!"

A *nuchshlepper* is there if you just got a big inheritance or won the lottery or bought a new condominium in Miami Beach. Just when you looked forward to spending a quiet time in the apartment, and you're moving in and you open the door and he's there. The *nuchshlepper*. You never told anyone you were moving in, but there he is. He's moving in, too.

You're sitting alone in a room and instead of one person to talk to, all of a sudden there's three people there, and none of them were invited. These are all *nuchshleppers*. They're the people who find out how much charm you have the day after they find out you just became a millionaire.

A *nuchshlepper* is like flypaper. When you become successful he is pasted to you. You can't get rid of him no matter how hard you try. He holds on to you for dear life. He can't make a living himself and the minute he learns that you do, he sticks all over you.

A *nuchshlepper* is like a mailman. He'll follow you through snow or heat or rain or dark of night. He'll follow you through blizzards, through fires, he'll never stop following you wherever you go, as long as you have money.

Every time you're invited to a wedding, the *nuchshlepper* shows up. By the time you get there, he's already dancing with the bride. You bring the gift and he eats the food.

Before you buy a new car, he's picked out the color. Any time you're packing for a trip, he's waiting at the airport. No matter when you arrive, the *nuchshlepper* is behind you.

You make reservations at a restaurant and by the time

you get there, he's already ordering. He's never invited, you never know how he found out, but he's always there, and no matter where you sit he's sitting next to you. Except when the check comes. That's the only time the *nuchshlepper* is not around, nowhere to be seen. The only way to get rid of a *nuchshlepper* is to call for the check.

After the meal, though, when you're sitting in your car there he is in the back seat. "So what took you so long?" he says. "Let's go!"

Ongeblozzen:
pronounced, OHN-geh-blozn

Someone who is *ongeblozzen* puffs himself up and walks around as if he owns the world.

A person who is *ongeblozzen* has his nose so far up in the air he can't find it. And he always has to top everybody. If you said you just had tea with the deputy prime minister of India, he tells you he just went hunting with the king of Siam. If you tell him a joke, he says he's got two better ones. He's always got a big deal going, and he's always on a telephone, either when you visit him at home or ride in his car or when he walks into your office. He says, "Can I make a call?" And he's always talking loud into the receiver: "Four million for what? I'm not going over three and a half million. He can take it or leave it! It's my final offer!" Then he hangs up. You don't have the heart to tell him that your phone has been disconnected since last week.

105

Ongeshtopt:
pronounced, OHN-geh-shtopt

It means "stuffed up," and refers to someone who is very wealthy. It's rarely a compliment. The word often goes with *mit gelt* and the literal translation of *ongeshtopt mit gelt* is "stuffed up with money." He's stuffed like *gefilte fish*, but with cash. In other words, filthy rich, disgustingly rich.

It's really only someone who has more money than you have and you can't stand it. You're bitter and jealous. Instead of saying he's a wealthy man, you say he's *ongeshtopt*, he's fat with money. He has practically no room left for storing more, and you're getting sick. You're getting sick of his money. You can always tell when a guy is *ongeshtopt* because everybody around him is getting nauseated from it.

Nobody wants to believe that he made the money because of his brains. Nobody accepts the idea, because if you admit to yourself that he made it on intelligence then you have to ask yourself, "Why didn't I make it?" It makes you feel stupid that you're not *ongeshtopt*, too.

Those who aren't *ongeshtopt* wonder why they can't achieve the same thing. Instead they convince themselves that the guy is a moron. He got lucky. He did it by a fluke, by some weird accident or coincidence. Everybody who ever saw someone other than himself get rich says the same thing: "Got lucky." That's the most typical expression among Jews. "The man got lucky. Fell into it."

How do you fall into three thousand factories all over the world when you started without a quarter? The others always have the same excuse: "Yeah, he got people around him who know everything. He happened to fall in with the right people."

You ask, "Which people?"

"Who knows? He's the one who fell into it. Why are you asking me?"

"So why didn't you do the same thing?"

"You think it's easy to find those people? He happened to bump into them. You can't predict who'll bump into you. It's a matter of luck."

"Maybe he found them."

"Find them! You can't find people like that. I've been looking a whole lifetime for them. I can't find them in a lifetime? You don't find these people. They find *you*. They somehow fall into you. They fall. It's a falling crowd of people who fall on top of you. And if they don't fall you'll never live to see it."

That's all they know: "Falling and lucky." They fell into it, they fall on top of it, they fell on this, they fell on that. Since they now can claim it's a total accident, they can eliminate the possibility of brain power having anything to do with it.

People always like to louse up the person who they say is *ongeshtopt*. After all, if you're that rich they only want to satisfy themselves that you have to be selfish and ruthless to get that rich. "You know how selfish you have to be? My God! You've got to be a ruthless bastard. That man never had any respect for anybody."

You ask, "Did he ever hurt anybody?"

"Are you kidding? Is he going to get that rich without hurting people? You gotta step on millions of people before you get there."

"Who did he step on?"

"Who cares? But without stepping on people you can't get there."

If a guy opens a store and sells a pastrami sandwich, and

107

if people like the sandwich they'll always buy it. Now the guy makes a profit every time he sells a sandwich. "Who did he step on?" I ask them. "Did he step on the sandwich? He's selling a sandwich. Are you trying to tell me that nobody wants to buy anything unless you stepped on somebody before you sold it to him?"

It's always the same response: "Ech, the people fell on him, he fell on the sandwich, he stepped on the people and the people stepped on the sandwich. He's stepping and falling and crawling and banging." They can't admit that the guy just happened to know what he was doing.

They think that the guy who is *ongeshtopt* never deserved to be so successful, they think. He never was good to his mother, he hates his children, if not for him his father would still be living in Philadelphia, his mother would still be in Israel. He wiped out a whole family. They always call the guy the low bastard. Even when he crosses the street, they say, "Look how obnoxious he looks crossing the street." They don't like the way he sits, they don't like the way he stands up. If he looks sad, people say "good, he deserves to be sad." When he drives down the street in his car they hope it breaks down.

Landlords are always *ongeshtopt*. No matter how broke a landlord gets, he's always *ongeshtopt*. Nobody wants to believe that he's losing money. Of course he's not losing money because it happens people are paying him rent. The fact that they're paying rent instead of owning a house or condominium bothers every Jew. They say, "It's only a location. The landlord didn't put any merchandise in, he didn't improve it every week. He didn't buy a new air conditioner. The refrigerator is there for the last five years already."

The sight of a landlord is a contemptible thing to these

people. The tenant completely forgets that the building costs money to build. The tenant thinks the landlord got the building for nothing because he doesn't see him build it. By the time you move in, it's already there. And he gives you nothing. If you want to sleep, you have to bring your own bed. If you want to sit, you have to provide your own chairs. If you want to get dressed, you have to have your own clothes. All he gave you was empty space. And empty space looks like something you could get for nothing. So you walk in the street and you see empty spaces that you don't have to pay for. You say to yourself, "Why should I have to pay for it over there?" And that's when just the thought of the *ongeshtopt* landlord makes you crazy.

Oy Vey!:
rhymes with "boy day"

O y *vey*" means "my God!" It also is: "How do you like that!" "I can't believe it!" "To hell with it!" "It's impossible!" "I'm overwhelmed!" "I'm overcome!" "I don't know how I can live through this." "I don't know what's going to happen to me." "I don't know where I'm going from here." "For me it's all over."

Oy vey! is the ultimate Jewish expression. It encompasses every negative feeling any Jew has ever had. Any time you feel rejected, disgusted, disturbed, miserable, hateful, nauseated, antagonistic, bitter, violent, turbulent—no matter what the negative feeling is, there is one phrase that has always said it best for Jews from the beginning of time. That phrase is *"oy vey!"*

It's almost like a death, a death to the whole system. Whether it's a small misery, big misery, or the worst misery. The first reaction is always *"oy vey!"*

If you just found out that the stock market crashed or you found out your wife is cheating or she turned down the divorce or you lost your visitation rights to the children or a hammer fell on your foot or you discovered that there's no gas in the tank, no shirts in the closet, only one cuff link in the drawer, you can't find the other sock, you lost a bet, the plane just took off without you—the first thing a Jew always says is, *"Oy vey!"* No other words in life can describe his predicament better.

When you take a good look at your blind date and she just looks bad, it's always *"oy."* If she looks really bad, it's *"oy vey!"* If she's pretty, it's never *"oy vey."* It's "Thank God. How do you like that?" *"Gib a kuk."*—Give a look! You mean, "take a look at what's happening here. Oh boy!"

It's not *"oy vey!"* when you feel something wonderful deep in your heart and you're praying that it all doesn't blow up in your face. So when your blind date turns out to be the girl of your dreams, you say to yourself, "I hope my eyes are not deceiving me. I'd better give another look to make sure I got the right girl. I hope this is not a mistake. I hope she's got the right door. I hope she had the right number. I hope she took the right bus. I hope she doesn't get sick. I hope she doesn't pass away. I hope she just lives through the night. I hope things don't get any better than this. I don't care how much the dinner costs now. Thank God I had the time. Am I glad I didn't take the other date. Am I glad I didn't call the other number. Am I glad I didn't go for the one with money. I hope I don't have an accident before the evening is over. I hope I used the right cologne. I hope I smell as good as she looks. I hope her divorce is final. I hope her kids are out of town. I hope she had enough sleep last night. I hope she won't tell me she's not the kind to fool around. I hope she doesn't find out I have an accent."

So you get everything ready, you've spent all the money, it's 2:00 in the morning, the wine is on the table, and you say to her, "Would you like to go to my place?" She says, "You're not my type."

Your excitement was so violent, you were going out of your mind with anticipation, you were so overwhelmed with possibilities and now everything collapses and you scream the only words you can think of and the only words that sum up all of your frustration at this intense moment: *oy vey!*

Schlemiel and Schlemazel:
pronounced, shleh-MEEL and shleh-MAH-zel

There's a common definition that a *schlemiel* is someone who spills soup on people and a *schlemazel* is someone who gets soup spilled on him. I think that's a preposterous definition. A *schlemiel* and a *shlemazel* are the same person. Usually they go out together. They hang around together. Each term is another way of saying someone's a jerk, an idiot, a *putz*, a screwball, or a helpless, pathetic individual. They're both always at the wrong end of the totem pole. In short, they're both professional losers.

Whatever is wrong that can happen to him happens, and

for reasons he can't figure out. He's always caving in no matter how hard he tries. The light is green and he drives ahead and someone crashes into him. Everybody is always crashing into him, and he's always crashing into everybody. No matter how much in the right he is.

The *schlemiel* tells somebody to keep his mouth shut because the guy is only four feet tall and has the nerve to talk while the cantor's singing. It's just his luck that the little guy is a karate expert who grabs him by the throat and throws him through the window.

Then he tries to get up from the ground and all of a sudden a guy on crutches shows up. The *schlemiel* figures he'll be safe with him, but this guy hits him on the ear with his crutch. Another guy in a wheelchair comes along and pushes him down the street. No matter where he goes, he always lands on his head. He doesn't know how it happened, but he's wiped out again.

Even on his wedding night, when he gets all dressed up, his pants and jacket don't match. Or he forgot to take the vest out of the cleaners. He comes to get married and it's the wrong wedding; he followed the wrong rabbi. There were four catering halls in the building and he accidentally spent three hours in the wrong one. Or the bride changed her mind. All of a sudden he's standing at the altar all by himself. Even his family and the rabbi went home.

When a schlemiel gets on a bus, the driver goes on strike.

He's the guy who gets on a plane wanting to go to Oakland, California, and winds up in Auckland, New Zealand.

A typical example of a schlemiel is the guy who spends his whole life telling you what he should have done, could have said, what could have been, could have happened.

He's never in touch with reality. His feet are on the

ground, but his head is in the clouds. He's always waiting for a miracle to happen, no matter how improbable it is.

It's like a guy who turns on the water faucet and—boom!—water comes flooding out and he's nearly drowned. He says to himself, "How the hell did that happen? It's not supposed to work that way." He doesn't call anyone to fix the faucet, and he never figures out that it might be broken. And every time he's about to turn it on, the *schlemiel* says, "Not this time." That's when all the water hits him in the face again.

Schlock:
rhymes with "flock"

chlock is the cheapest, the lowest of anything. A man who deals in *schlock* has a *schlock* mentality. Any time you see anything you consider cheap, you say, "Ech, *schlock.*" It's low class.

A man says, "What do you think of that guy's coat? He just paid $3,000 for it."

His friend says, "It's *schlock.*"

But when you meet the person with the coat it's always, "*Oy,* what a stunning outfit. It's a fantastic outfit." But the name for every outfit, as soon as the person turns around, is, "*Schlock.* Imagine the nerve to even wear a coat like that."

You walk into someone's apartment and everybody says the same thing: "Gorgeous, stunning, unbelievable." But as soon as that person turns around everybody says "Who could

113

have an apartment like this? Did you ever see such drapes? And that table? Ay! A reject from the Salvation Army. I've never seen *schlock* like this in my whole life!"

Schlock is the great turn-around word for everything and everybody.

A certain kind of person has a *schlock* mentality. A guy never buys anything of value and rationalizes that he doesn't need it, would never have any use for it, and there's no place in the house to keep it. Basically, he's a cheap bastard.

He tries to pretend that everything that stinks is more comfortable or lasts longer or looks better. He would never buy a silk shirt because he says that silk sticks to your body. He wouldn't buy expensive shoes because they scruff easily. And he'd never be caught dead flying first class. "What do I need a bigger chair for?" he asks. "I don't have that big a back. I don't weigh seven hundred pounds. What am I, an elephant?"

If you ask him why he doesn't buy a new car, he tells you, "For what? They're too comfortable. Too much cushion. You sit down and you start falling asleep." He says that the *schlock* car he owns is actually saving his life. If he had a new car, I'd have passed away a week and a half ago.

Schmaltz:
pronounced, Schmahlts

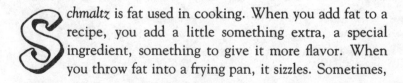

chmaltz is fat used in cooking. When you add fat to a recipe, you add a little something extra, a special ingredient, something to give it more flavor. When you throw fat into a frying pan, it sizzles. Sometimes, there's more sizzle than substance, so the word is occasionally used as a substitute for hokey. But mostly, for Jews, *schmaltz* has come to be associated with depicting somebody with warmth or pizzazz or the ability to give or express love. It is a way of ascribing somebody, or something, with life.

If a guy who has a drab personality goes to buy a suit, he wants it to have some life because he doesn't. This guy has a personality that came right out of a computer. So he wants something snazzy to wear, and the salesman sees right away the guy's a drip, so he takes a colorless suit from the rack that he hasn't been able to move in four years, puts it on the guy, and says, "Ah, this has *schmaltz!*"

You take your wife to buy a jacket. She wants one that will stop traffic, so she picks out an expensive one. You're not such a big spender to begin with, and you'd just as soon not have her buy this jacket. So the best way to discourage her is to look the jacket over when she's trying it on and say: "Got no *schmaltz.*" It doesn't always work, but it's a good try.

To a Jew, for something to be worthwhile, for something to work, it has to have that something extra. Jews see it as warmth. Someone could be running for office and he talks about the deficit, disarmament, the budget and the stealth bomber. The average Jewish voter says about the candidate, "Forget defense. You can always get defense. What I want to know is, does he have *schmaltz?*"

Schmeer:
rhymes with "beer"

This is a payoff or a bribe.

A *schmeer* is related to when a guy swears that something is impossible, it will never come to pass, just forget about it. But show him the right price for something and see what happens. Suddenly anything is possible. Somehow, in some unbelievable way, miracles happen. That's a tribute to the significance of money in society.

Everybody is familiar with the procedure in restaurants. You can't get a reservation. Everything is booked up. There's no place to put another person or another table or another chair or even a toothpick. There's absolutely no room, but show the maitre d' $8 and it's amazing how in an instant there's room all over the building. The maitre d' doesn't know where it came from, how it happened, or where everything else went. But suddenly the room is made for you. It's like a construction company came in and put up another building in twelve seconds.

I think it was at the Copacabana where the saying about a *schmeer* was invented. Frank Sinatra is on stage singing his main number and there's no room anywhere in the club. All of a sudden a table materializes for your party right in front of him, and you're sitting there. You're so close to Frank Sinatra that you're staring at his crotch. You were never in show business until you had the right price, and now you're in the middle of the stage. Meanwhile the maitre d' does the same thing for one party after another, and before you know it, there's no room left for Frank Sinatra. *He* has to move, he winds up singing "Be My Love" from the toilet. Out on the stage they're still adding more tables.

116

Schmuck:
||||||||||||||||||||||||||||||||||||
rhymes with "cluck"

Most people don't know the literal meaning of the word *schmuck*. They usually use it as the equivalent of a jerk, but the word comes from the German word for jewel. The phrase "family jewel" is a colloquialism or euphemism for the male sexual organ. So when someone is called a *schmuck*, he's actually being called a penis, or a *putz*, which is a Yiddish synonym for *schumck*. People are correct in using it as a put-down word, like the word "bastard" in English.

In English, you're not necessarily saying that a guy was literally born out of wedlock when you call him a bastard. Some bastards—those truly born out of wedlock—can of course be wonderful people, just like anyone else. But actual bastards were once ostracized from society, and were considered contemptible, and were generally unacceptable. But today it has nothing to do with the original translation.

Just like the word *momzer* in Yiddish, which is literally "bastard." It's generally used in a more angry tone than is the word *schmuck*. But again, no one is really saying that the guy they're calling a bastard is legally a bastard. He's just a bastard in the other person's eyes.

When you call a guy a bastard, or a *momzer*, you're saying the man's an idiot, he's a jerk, he's a goof, he's a lowlife, he's a real good-for-nothing *schmuck*.

Schnorrer:
pronounced, SHNORR-er

A *schnorrer* is a chiseler, a moocher, a beggar, but a resourceful one; he spends his whole life figuring out how to live off other people. He's not successful unless he feels he can make his way through life for nothing. It's below cheap.

A *karga mensh* means a cheap person, but at least he pays something. The *schnorrer* doesn't want to go in his pocket for a dime. A *karga mensh* will go to a theater and buy seats in the highest balcony and in the last row because they cost the least. A *schnorrer* calls the star of the show and says, "Do you mind if my wife and seven children and my mother-in-law come to your show tonight?" The star says, "Mind? Who am I to keep you out if you want to buy tickets?" The *schnorrer* says, "Buy? You don't give for free? We know each other all our lives and from such an old friend you want money?"

A *schnorrer* is also different from a *nuchshlepper* in that he doesn't hang on you quite as much because he pretends to have a little more dignity. But he always happens to materialize when you take out your wallet. A *schnorrer* is different from a *chozzer* in that a *schnorrer* not only tries to take all he can, but he insults you while he does it.

Shanda:
pronounced, SHAHN-duh

Shanda means "embarrassment;" but it's actually worse than that. It's something to be ashamed of, a deep humiliation.

A husband is putting on a tuxedo to attend a wedding and looks at himself in the mirror and says, "It's perfect!" The wife says, "But a plaid tuxedo? Whoever saw a plaid tuxedo? Maybe for a gentile on a boat ride. But for a Jewish wedding? It's a _shanda._"

"It's a _shanda_ for the neighbors," is a common usage. You want your son to become a doctor and one day he comes home and announces, "Hello, forget about being a doctor, I decided to become a plumber." "_Oy_, my son the plumber. It's a _shanda_ for the neighbors."

It used to be that the worst crime any Jewish son could commit was to marry a _shiksa_, a girl who isn't a Jew. The parents would be ashamed to be seen any place. "How can we go anywhere? How is the family going to face anybody? I'd rather be hit by a streetcar. _Oy_, it's a _shanda._"

Jewish families all know each other and, as it happens, they are always competing. Who marries whom, who has what, who bought what. If everybody has a big, beautiful refrigerator and you still have an ice box, it is an embarrassment. By the time everybody had a toilet in the house, and you still had to go the communal toilet in the hall, _that's_ a _shanda._

The same goes with a car. Jewish cars go up a grade every ten years. Thirty years ago a Jew was proud if he even owned a car. Twenty years ago, it was a great thing to have a _new_ car. Ten years ago, every Jew had to have a Cadillac. Now a

Jew is a *putz* unless he has a Mercedes. In some neighborhoods, if he's a young Jew, he has to have a BMW. You can't be seen anymore with anything less.

If a Jew wants to go to a restaurant without his wife or threatens to have a good time anywhere, that becomes a *shanda*. She says, "You know how it looks to be seen anywhere in the world without me? Everybody else has his wife with him and I won't be there? You know what they're going to say? Where's your wife? You're going to tell them that I'm not there? It's a *shanda!*"

When a Jew puts on a jacket, you can bet his wife is probably going to say, "You call that a jacket? I call it a *shanda*." The only time she doesn't think so, no matter how cheap the jacket is, is when she wants to buy a mink coat. Then the jacket is good enough. All of a sudden, it's not a *shanda* because now she's trying to get the money for the fur coat from him.

"I don't mind if I don't have a mink coat" she says. To me, it looks fine to wear that old *shmatte* I have, but you know how it looks for *you* if I don't have a mink coat?" That's the ultimate *shanda*. "Do you know how *you* look to people if *I* don't have a mink coat?" She doesn't want the mink for herself, she doesn't need it. Every woman who ever wanted a mink coat says the same thing: "Do you think *I* want a mink coat? You think *I* need a mink coat? You think *I* care if I don't have a mink coat? It's not for me, it's for *you*."

The same thing happens when a wife wants a Mercedes. She says, "Do you think *I* need a Mercedes? I couldn't care less. But how does it look for your business if you don't have a Mercedes?" The fact is, after he buys the Mercedes he'll never live to see that car again. If by some chance he does, it'll be because he took a bus to the beauty parlor.

Shlog Zich Kop in Vant:
pronounced, shlogh zikh kohp in VAHNT

It means "go hit your head against the wall." You use it when something seems useless, it seems like it will never happen, and if you worry about it, it'll do as much good as if you knock your head against the wall. It means spending a lot of time and energy on nothing. Like worrying whether or not your house will become an airplane. Or hoping the landlord won't come for the rent. In fact, I heard that expression in my house all the time when I told my parents that I wanted to become a comedian. The next words were: *Go hit your head against the wall.*

For members of my family, the idea of somebody from a poverty-stricken neighborhood like the Lower East Side becoming an actor or a star or someone successful in show business seemed as remote as if I had said I was going to become the emperor of Ethiopia.

When everybody in my family found out that I wanted to become a comedian, they all said the same thing, *"Shlog zich kop in vant."* My brothers said it, my mother, my father, cousins, aunts, the janitor of the building, the lady on the stoop—all said it. Somebody screamed it from a window on the third floor, someone else shouted from the cellar. If I said hello in a restaurant, and anybody from my family was there, they would tell it to the waitress and then she told me off! And so did the three busboys from Puerto Rico. Everybody told me off.

Nobody in the neighborhood could relate to doing anything outside the neighborhood. Anything else was just something you heard on the radio. If you didn't use it in person, then it didn't exist. They considered things in only the narrowest terms, and so a large ambition was not only unattainable, it was impractical. This was the view of people who considered the customer peddler the most successful guy in the area.

The customer peddler walked around with three dresses and two shirts and four belts in a cardboard box because he couldn't afford a valise. He sold his few clothes from house to house. All the clothes were paid for on credit because nobody could afford to buy a shirt or even a belt for cash. This was before credit cards, and you gave the guy a quarter towards the shirt and paid it out for the next four and a half years. The shirt was worn out three years ago and you were still paying for it. This customer peddler, because he got a quarter from each person here and there, was the richest guy in the neighborhood.

So people aspired either to be a peddler or a rabbi, in order to even have a chance to make any kind of living. But a comedian? "Ha! Go take your head and hit it against the wall!"

Shmatte:
‖‖‖‖‖‖‖‖‖‖‖‖‖‖‖‖‖‖‖‖‖‖‖‖‖‖‖
pronounced, SHMOT-ta

*S*hmatte, "rag," is a word that could be used either as a compliment or as an insult. If a woman is talking about what another woman is wearing, it's a *shmatte*. If she happens to own that same dress, it's *couture*. When a woman wants her husband to buy her more clothes, then everything she owns suddenly becomes a *shmatte*. Everything in her closet overnight becomes a *shmatte*. She says to her husband, "You want your wife to be seen in public with *shmattes* like these?"

A *shmatte* to a wife is also everything her husband is wearing. It's most often used after the husband gets dressed. No matter what he's got on, she says, "You're not ashamed to walk down the street with a *shmatte* like that? Is that all you have to put on? What, you don't care?"

When a Jewish woman is in a dress store and sees that they've raised the price for something ten times the original amount, then all of a sudden it goes from being a *shmatte* to high fashion. You give her the right label and it's not a *shmatte* anymore. No matter how beautiful a dress is, if it has an unknown name it's a *shmatte*. But all she has to see is an Italian or French label, then immediately it's *couture*. They don't buy clothes, they buy labels. If you sold them enough labels you don't need any clothes at all. Most Jewish women would be happy to walk around in nothing but labels.

Why do you think it is that every time you say hello to a Jew you end up reading for an hour and a half? It's because they have labels on every item in the world. They don't care if it doesn't fit. That's not important. If it has the right label, *that's* what counts.

Let's assume the hottest item today is a pair of jeans. It's the name on those jeans that becomes stylish. Ordinarily jeans would be considered a *shmatte*, a rag to clean the floor with. It would be considered *tseharget*—falling apart—because the jeans are faded or they're torn. But ten minutes later, because it has the right label, it's a hot item. Eighty-year-old Jewish women are walking around with torn jeans on Fifth Avenue and they call it *couture*.

Shpilkes:
pronounced, SHPILL-kess

Someone with *shpilkes* is someone who has no patience, who is always in a hurry, and who always has to be on his way. "What are you, on *shpilkes?*" *Shpilkes* is impatience to the highest degree. If you tell a guy with *shpilkes* a story, he can't wait for you to finish. He says, "Get to the punch line already. What's taking so long?"

He can't wait to get a dial tone on the telephone. He gulps down his soup in a restaurant and is impatient for you to finish. He's a super-restless maniac. If you ask someone with *shpilkes* why he's in such a hurry, he doesn't know, except that he feels somehow or other that life is passing him by. He constantly imagines that there is real action in some other place that he must get to.

He's always running across the street, dodging traffic, and risking his life to get to the other side. Whenever he's in a car, he's always honking his horn because he feels the guy in front of him is holding him back. When he gets to where he's going, he winds up doing the same thing that he did before: absolutely nothing. And he's just as impatient in the new place.

Someone with *shpilkes* is constantly asked the question, *"Bist ahf ain fus?"* It means "are you in a hurry?" The literal translation gives you the picture of this character: "Are you standing on one leg?"

124

Shtick:
rhymes with "stick"

A *shtick* is a piece, a bit, or a lump. Any comedy material is always called *shtick*. Anything that's organized into a comedic piece of business is a *shtick*. You're teasing somebody, it's a *shtick*. If a guy is making fun of you, it's a *shtick*: "Watch this *shtick*." If I walked over to Mike Tyson and threatened to punch him in the mouth, that would be called a *shtick*. And you'd better make sure *he* knows it's a *shtick*.

Shtick has become a popular term in show business, even with gentiles. When they want to refer to a routine that someone does, to identify a person with his material, they say, "That's his *shtick*." When Danny Kaye talked in that fast singsong nonsense, that was his *shtick*. When Jack Benny stood there and just looked and didn't say a word, that was his *shtick*.

A *shtick* also means a joke. If a man gives you a check for $1 million for the shirt off your back, don't try to cash it because you can bet your life it's a *shtick*. A *shtick* could be a practical joke. It could be when a man pulls a chair out when you're about to sit down. You break your head, you're bleeding like a pig, but the guy will tell you it's not his fault because it was a *shtick*. He was just playing.

You hear the word when children hit the grandfather in the head with a toy. To the grandfather it's a calamity because he's almost passing away from the pain. But to the parents of the kid, they say, "It's a *shtick*, it's a *shtick*. He was only kidding."

When you're trying to be funny, whether it works or not, it's called a *shtick*. That's supposed to justify anything; it's the great escape.

Tchotchke:
pronounced, CHOCH-keh

tchotchke is a toy, but in common usage it is not meant strictly to refer to an actual toy. It's often used in regard to a person that you love. Like, "That's my *tchotchke*." It means "I'm fond of her the way a child is crazy about a toy." You're describing a feeling. A child relates to toys, that's why a doll becomes a living thing to a child. And when a man or woman calls his sweetheart "doll," it is usually said with the greatest affection.

A *tchotchke* is also used for a nice-looking young female, a pretty little number, someone you may not take too seriously but that you'd like not to do without. "Oy, what a *tchotchke* he found!" "Wouldn't you like to have a *tchotchke* like that to fool around with?" "What a *tchotchke*—if only I could afford it!"

Toches Lekker:
pronounced, TAW-khess lek-ker

When someone kisses someone's behind in order to gain favors, this is a *toches lekker*. A *toches lekker* is the king of the *nuchshleppers*—people who latch onto successful people—because this *nuchshlepper* is the one who is outdistancing all the others. If you can't get away fast enough from the head *nuchshlepper*, then you're feeling a *toches lekker*.

126

Toyten Bankes:
pronounced, TOY-ten BAHN-kess

L iterally speaking, *toyten bankes* means that there's no chance you can get anywhere with what you're doing. In plain English, it's going to do you as much good as riding a dead horse.

Toyten bankes comes from the old custom of bleeding a sick person in an attempt to relieve or reduce fever. *Bankes* refers to the suction cup used for bleeding the sick, for making the blood rise to the surface of the skin. *Toyten* means dead. And so the saying is "no matter what you do, it will help as much as cupping will help a corpse."

Toyten bankes is a hopeless case. It's like trying to talk your son out of marrying a gorgeous *shiksa*. You first try to appeal to religious convictions or how it violates all the traditional principles. But why he's attracted to her has nothing to do with religion. What he wants from her is nothing you're going to find in a temple. So compared to his sex drive, religion is going to help like a *toyten bankes*. What he wants from her is so uncontrollable that even if God himself showed up he wouldn't know where to turn for help. The Bible in the motel room says, "Thou shalt not," but when she says, "I'm ready," the Bible doesn't have a chance.

Another instance is when you see a girl you're wild about. She's wearing a mink coat and she's getting into a Rolls Royce. Some guy is taking her on a ten-day cruise. You rush over and tell her that if you had more money you'd buy her the world. You tell her that *he* might have more money and *he* might look better but you have something that *he* could never give her. She asks, "What?" You say, "Wisdom." Then they drive

127

off. If you had any real wisdom, you'd know that that line would help you like a *toyten bankes.*

Someone in the real estate business is trying to sell his condominium in Staten Island, but no one has bought a condominium there in sixteen years. He says, "I've got an idea. I'll put in a swimming pool. I'll put in a tennis court. I'll get a doorman." His friend says, "Forget it, Harold. It's a *toyten bankes.*"

You grab the guy and tell him, "Look, it's a two-million-dollar condominium, and I'll sell it to you for three hundred dollars. It's the biggest bargain in history." He's beating a dead horse. If the real estate guy had any intelligence, he'd understand that a Jew on Flatbush Avenue wouldn't have the slightest interest in a condominium in Staten Island, no matter how cheap it was. He tells you, "There's no way to send your kids to Hebrew school in Staten Island. And who can get married there? Do you know how long you have to look before you find a rabbi for a ceremony? Do you know how big Staten Island is? Stop kidding yourself. It's a *toyten bankes.*"

A Jew gets a VCR and is trying to figure out how to work it. He gets a manual and reads it from start to finish twenty-five times. And he still can't work the machine. He could spend a thousand hours at it. He could be trying to understand the thing from the time he was eight years old until he was seventy-three. It doesn't matter. He's still on the floor trying to figure it out. He'll never learn it because it's a *toyten bankes.*

Trafe:
rhymes with "safe"

This literally is something that is not kosher to eat, that is forbidden by the orthodox dietary laws. Jews, however, extend the use of the word into their personal relationships. If somebody wants to talk you out of something, he says, "Don't go near it, it's *trafe.*" They used to say that a *shiksa*—a gentile girl—is *trafe*: "Don't touch her." There's the old joke that there's no mercy or decency or justice in this world because whenever a guy sees a stunning *shiksa*, he says, "That's *trafe* and my wife is *kosher?*"

To take a gentile girl on a date costs a dollar and a quarter, or it costs nothing. It was the price of sitting down on a park bench. With a Jewish girl you always have to take her someplace. So all of a sudden she becomes a problem to you. Every Jewish girl wants to know what restaurant you are taking her to, and whether there will be celebrities eating nearby. She knows the menu backwards and forwards and what the highest-priced items are. She wants Jewish men to cater to her because going on a date, in her mind, is like a catered affair. And God forbid you should take a bus, or even a taxi. She always asks where the limousine is. Even before you get on the date you're defending yourself because she thinks you're a cheap bastard. If a limousine doesn't show up, she'll leave you at 8:30.

A *shiksa*, though, is used to standing at the counter. If you get her a seat in a coffee shop with a cushion, you are a big hit. If you buy her a pack of cigarettes and put fifty cents in the jukebox, you are a big spender.

But still the gentile girl is considered *trafe* because there is always the fear that you might get involved with her. To marry a gentile is considered close to passing away.

129

In order to control you, everybody in your family will say, "It's *trafe*, stay away from her." She became like eating bacon or ham, or ordering a lobster.

Trombenik:
pronounced, TROM-beh-nick

A *trombenik* is an irresponsible guy who's not working and is a swinger or a playboy. He has no visible source of income. He's a bum, he's no good, and usually he's having a much better time than anybody else.

Tsebruchen, Tseharget:
pronounced, zhe-BROOKH-en, zhe-HAR-get

If you really want to louse somebody up, this is a way of saying it. It's saying that somebody looks and resembles nothing. But in Yiddish, when they want to say that a person really looks bad, and they want to dig deep down to draw out the best insults they can, they make it sound like the man is totally collapsing, they say *tsebruchen, tseharget. Tsebruchen* means broken down and *tseharget* means falling

130

apart. It's a double dose. "He's *tsebruchen, tseharget.*" It means he looks like a car crash.

Tsebruchen, tseharget is in fact used a lot in the sense of an automobile accident. When you were first hit by the car it didn't feel like much, but when it's time to make a case out of it, now that's different. If you're trying to collect $100,000, it's *tsebruchen.* But if you're trying to collect $1 million, every bone in your body is broken. It's *tsebruchen, tseharget.*

Jews are not content to say that something just looks bad. It has to look terrible, disgusting, loathesome, so destroyed that it's not even human anymore; it's on the level of a cockroach. It's like when a guy approaches a beautiful girl and makes a play for her. But if she tells him to take a walk, he suddenly didn't want her in the first place. But then he has to louse her up as much as possible. The same girl that was a beauty five seconds ago is all of a sudden transformed. He says, "Who wants her? What a mess. She's falling apart in every direction."

His friend then says, "But wait, you just said she was beautiful." The guy says, "That was from here, but I didn't see her up close. Up close you should see what she looks like." "Like what?" "*Tsebruchen, tseharget.*"

If you're at your wit's end with catastrophe, you might even say, *tsebruchen, tseharget, tsecruchen, tsetuchen,* which means something is not only breaking and falling apart, as in the first two words, but it's also cracking and crumbling and it just got a bunch of holes punched in it, too.

131

Untershmeichlin:
pronounced, oonter-SHMY-khlin

This means to butter somebody up. To smear a little something on him. The *nuchshlepper*—a leech to the rich and influential—always acts out a little *untershmeichlin* to insure his hold. This is his field of expertise. He's giving as many compliments as possible in every direction in order to be allowed to stick around. He figures that if he gives you enough compliments, if he can butter up enough sides of you, he'll never have to go to work again.

Yenta:
pronounced, YEHN-teh

A *yenta* is a woman who is always talking about someone else's business. She never does anything herself, but she's always working over everybody else who is doing something. A *yenta* is never involved in a situation herself because she's too busy finding out what's going on in your life and talking about it to other people.

If somebody gets sick, a *yenta* won't tell you how sick he is, but she'll tell you he wouldn't have been sick if not for his sister. Or he wouldn't have suffered a relapse if not for his doctor. And his house wouldn't be in bad shape if not for his plumber. His toilet would run better if not for his cousins. His daughter would be a better dancer if not for the teacher.

132

He would be making a fortune if not for his partner. He wouldn't have converted if not for his wife, and everybody would still be living if not for her cooking.

With a *yenta* nothing is ever right. She'll always tell you why everybody is wrong and what's wrong with them. She's always telling stories, but there's never a good side to any of them. She never happens to hear the good side or doesn't want to hear it. Or never repeats it. It's boring to her. The only thing that interests her is who died, who's getting killed, who's killing somebody, who's getting divorced, who's getting destroyed. A *yenta* gets nauseated from hearing good news. To her good news is worthless. It might as well never have happened at all.

No matter how great a house looks, somehow or other the *yenta* hates it. You can walk into a $90 million house and everybody says it's the most stunning place in the world, but the *yenta* says, "Yeah, but who would want to live here?" She's walking around with a finger, touching every piece of furniture for dust. No matter what she touches, she always says the same thing: "Yeech. You call this a house? How could a person spend five minutes in a place like this?" If it's beautiful, it's filthy. If it's got three hundred rooms, she won't say it's fantastic because it's got so much room. She says it's impossible to live there because you can get lost. She says, "How could you talk to somebody if you don't know where they are?"

You could buy the most beautiful silk shirt in the world. The *yenta* will say, "So what? It falls apart in a minute."

You live among shrubbery and she says, "Fresh air is the worst thing in the world for you. It makes you breathe a lot."

If you have a chauffeur with a limousine, she'll say, "Yeech, it's terrible." What's terrible? "Who could stand a person following you around the whole day?"

Yichus:
pronounced, YIKH-ess

Yichus means your lineage, your heritage, or your family tree. It has the sense of nobility, prestige, pedigree. When people amounted to nothing, they always wanted their children to marry into a prominent family. Usually the head of the family with the status was an important rabbi or a noted surgeon. Or the family could be the lowest mess in the world but they had a lot of money. A lot of money and true accomplishment were comparable.

A family might be poor, but if it had a rabbinical tradition, then that's great. That's *yichus*. If you can't get a historical family of rabbis, the next best thing is to find some person with a lot of money. Then you can leave out the rabbi altogether. You're willing to convert if it's the right amount. Once you have enough money, then where you got it isn't important.

If you're John Dillinger's daughter, it doesn't matter if your father was the one who left you all her money. You've got *yichus*. Same with Al Capone and Meyer Lansky. It doesn't matter that both were thought of as mass murderers, they were rich mass murderers. Morality is the most important issue to outsiders unless the other people are rich. This is not only Jewish, this is for every denomination, every race, every nationality.

Nobody ever asks a wealthy person how he made his money. They only know that he has it. If you judge most of the millionaires in this country by how they made their fortune, it would usually draw disrespect, contempt, and hate, because most of the major wealth of the world was made through thievery. There are exceptions, but not many.

134

The billionaires of today are lower than such "robber barons" as the original Rockefellers or Vanderbilts. Every munitions maker, every defense department manufacturer has a sweetheart of a crooked deal. They're either manufacturing bullets that don't work, planes that don't fly, or tanks that can't move. Those items that do work are killing people every day and the owners are making millions, and these people are considered the benefactors of society.

Yosher:
||||||||||||||||||||||||||||||
pronounced, YOH-shur

*Y*osher means decency. It's showing compassion and it's having sympathy. *Yosher* implies: Don't try to take advantage of people; don't try to take advantage of a situation.

For example, you pick up the check every time you see someone. One day you say to him, "*Yosher*. What would be so bad if one time you picked up the check?"

It's when you think the other person is being totally unfair. "Don't you think you should have a little *yosher*?"

The boss hasn't given you a raise in five years. You ask him about it and he says, "What do you need a raise for all of a sudden?" You say, "Don't you think you should show a little *yosher*? Do I have to wait until I've passed away, God forbid, before I get a raise?"

You give your brother-in-law $30,000 to open a restaurant. Then the restaurant, after it opens, is not doing so hot, so he calls you to help pay the rent. You tell him, "It's bad

135

enough I put you in business, now I have to pay your rent, too? *Yosher,* how much are you going to ask somebody for? Isn't there any limit?"

Your mother-in-law comes to stay for a weekend and she's still there a month later. You complain to your wife, who says, "She's my mother. Don't pick on her." And you say, "So, *yosher?*" As if to say, "When is the van coming? Don't you think you could show a little compassion for my point of view? Don't I count, too? Are you the only person involved in this relationship? I'm here, too. *Yosher,* what am I, *chopped liver?*"

Zhlub:
rhymes with "tub"

A *zhlub* is a guy who could make a new suit look like a *shmatte.* No matter what he wears or how successful he becomes, he still looks like a failure.

His coat never fits, his tie always has stains, and if you stand too close to him when he talks, you always know he's just eaten onions. He's a coarse guy, without any grace in his speech or his movements.

A *zhlub* is still walking around by the food table when the *bar mitzvah* is over and eating scraps with his fingers. When he's full he takes pieces of cake and puts them into his shopping bag. He's left over longer than the leftovers.

A *zhlub* will go to a wedding and kiss the groom instead of the bride. If a traffic cop stops him, he wouldn't try to talk

136

his way out of a ticket, but he'd tell the cop off, and then get two tickets.

A *zhlub* is not nuts, but he's not normal, either. He laughs too loud. When he goes to a movie, everybody turns around and looks at him. Everybody knows he's making a *schmuck* out of himself except him. He's the type of guy who would walk around with a Jewish flag at an Arab parade. He's an innocent person; he's not calculating. Basically, he's more pathetic than mean.

A *zhlub* is the irrelevant guy at every affair. The waiter always misses him when he's serving. No matter what he does, the *zhlub* doesn't make any difference. He's so insignificant that his boss doesn't even know he's working for him. That's why the *zhlub* never gets fired. They can't fire him because they don't know who he is, and nobody ever heard of him before.

A *zhlub* will go to a funeral and be the only one to tell a joke because he thinks it's the only way to compensate for the mourners' grief. Even though he might have love in his heart, he still creates bad feelings. Even when he tells a girl he loves her, she could swear he doesn't mean it because it was the wrong time and the wrong place to say it.

A *zhlub* doesn't try to offend, it just comes naturally. When he looks in the mirror, he can't believe his luck that he's such a charming person.